A Jewish Christmas Story

A Jewish Christmas Story

Frank Straight

Scripture taken from the HOLY BIBLE, NEW INTERNATIONAL VERSION [R].
Copyright[C] 1973, 1978, 1984 by International Bible Society. Used by permission
of Zondervan. All rights reserved.

Scripture taken from The Message. Copyright [C] 1993, 1994, 1995, 1996, 2000,
2001, 2002. Used by permission of NavPress Publishing Group.

This book was printed in the United States of America.

To order additional copies of this book, contact:
Xlibris Corporation
1-888-795-4274
www.Xlibris.com
Orders@Xlibris.com
68806

DEDICATION

This book is dedicated to the one person who has patiently sat through almost all of the Bible classes I have taught, including many repeats, and not answered my puzzling questions so others could try and has answered when everyone else gave up!
Thanks Janice, wife and best in class!

A JEWISH CHRISTMAS STORY

MATTHEW CHAPTERS 1 AND 2

INTRODUCTION

(What Does It All Mean?)

A Jewish father was troubled by the way his son turned out, and went to see his Rabbi about it. "I brought him up in the faith, gave him a very expensive bar mitzvah, cost me a fortune to educate him. Then he tells me last week he has decided to be a Christian! Rabbi, where did I go wrong?"

"Funny you should come to me," said the Rabbi. "Like you, I too, brought my boy up in the faith, put him through University, cost me a fortune, then one day he, too, tells me he has decided to become a Christian."

"What did you do?" asked the father.

"I turned to God for the answer" replied the Rabbi.

"And what did he say?" pressed the father.

"God said, 'Funny you should come to me . . . '"

"A Jewish Christmas Story" sounds like a contradiction. Jewish folks do not usually go in for Christmas much. They might be surprised that there is such a thing as a Jewish Christmas Story! Perhaps you are also surprised. If we put aside most of what passes for "Christmas" in our 21st century, and consider the birth of Jesus as the Bible presents it (at one time in the distant past Christmas seems to have been about the birth of Jesus!), we have two accounts to read. These are in Matthew and Luke's Gospels. And Matthew is considered a Gospel intended especially for, of all people, Jews! Oh, yes. The person whose birth is supposed to be the "reason for the season" just happens to be Jewish! So, we will look in Matthew's Gospel for "A Jewish Christmas Story."

In the first two chapters of Matthew's Gospel, he tells about the birth and infancy of Jesus. Christians and even unbelievers are familiar with many of the events Matthew describes. The "three wise men" and the mysterious star which guided them have been made famous in Christmas carols and Christmas pageants which are sung and presented every December. "O Little Town of Bethlehem" gains its fame for celebrating the village which is the predicted birthplace in Matthew's narrative.

Other parts of Matthew's story are not so well known and sometimes seem puzzling to the casual reader. Matthew starts with a long list of mostly unfamiliar names which are difficult to pronounce and seldom ever actually read. He even includes women in his genealogy. What is that all about?

Why was Jesus' birth considered by many to be a scandal? Were Joseph and Mary really married or just engaged when the special child was born? Matthew describes Jesus as having four different "fathers". What does he mean by this? What is a "Magi" and why are they so prominent in Matthew's story? Did they start the whole Christmas gift giving frenzy? Could any one be so cruel as to kill the innocents as Herod supposedly did? Why would this be part of a "Christmas" story? To some extent Matthew's story is a narrative about places; Jerusalem, Bethlehem, Rama, Egypt, and Nazareth are all mentioned. Why so much geography? And, by the way, Matthew quotes a lot from the Old Testament. Is this significant?

What, in fact, does it all mean?

It seems that Matthew's description of the birth of the Messiah has been mostly used as a source for Christmas music and for plays usually performed by children. This has become a way to keep the story of the birth of Jesus active in our consciousness, at least during one season of the year. This has been a worthy, if unintended, outcome of Matthew's writing. It is certain, however, that this was not Matthew's main purpose. He wrote his Gospel, his "Good News", to tell his readers about Jesus Christ. His intent was the same as Luke who wrote at the beginning of Acts: **Acts 1:1** "In my former book, (His Gospel) Theophilus, I wrote about all that Jesus began to do and to teach."

In telling about Jesus, I believe Matthew strives in the birth story to make sure the reader understands who Jesus is and what his purposes are. The birth story is an integral part of Matthew's Gospel. This Gospel includes the parables of Jesus, his miracles, sayings, preaching and prayers, and is studied diligently. The birth story in the first two chapters should be given the same serious study.

The purpose of this study book is to help the student understand what Matthew is telling us in his birth narrative. What does it all mean? There are eight chapters which can be used in the weeks preceding the Christmas celebration. Hopefully, the study can bring a more serious experience to a Christmas season which in many respects is now dominated by rampant commercialism.

With any study of the Bible, we must read, study and seek input from Godly scholars. (Paul "sat at the feet" of Gamaliel, a prominent Jewish teacher!) And most importantly, we have to ask the Holy Spirit to guide our understanding. Using this approach, I put forward understandings of Matthew's narrative which make sense to me and seem consistent with the overall intent of his Gospel. Others may come to different understandings of Matthew's intent which could be equally helpful.

It is my hope that the reader of this study will come to appreciate Matthew's teaching in the first two chapters of his Gospel in a new and better way, and that, in knowing Jesus more fully, be inclined to share and serve him with greater enthusiasm.

At the conclusion of each chapter are 8-10 questions about the material covered in the chapter. It is intended that these be used to review what has been presented and to deepen the reader's understanding of the birth story. Some of the questions do not have simple, short answers (the dreaded essay question!). Consequently, in a group setting, I hope they can promote fruitful discussions.

The author's answers to the Study Questions can be found at the back of the study guide in an APPENDIX. They have been placed in this separate section because these answers have been used to expand and amplify the information in the eight chapters of the study guide. **It is strongly suggested that the reader prepare his or her own answers to the questions before consulting the APPENDIX.**

It is noted that all scripture references in the guide are in bold print. The purpose of this is to emphasize the importance of reading, knowing and understanding **the Scriptures.**

All Scripture references are from the New International Version (NIV) unless noted otherwise.

—Frank Straight

CONTENTS

Rejoice!

CHAPTER 1

WHOSE SON IS HE?

*"To forget one's ancestors is to be a brook without a source,
a tree without a root." Chinese Proverb*

Matthew 1:1 ¹A record of the genealogy of Jesus Christ the son of David, the son of Abraham:

 The first verse of the First Gospel says that Jesus Christ is the son of David and the son of Abraham. Matthew goes on to explain in his birth story how and why Joseph would come to be known as Jesus' Father. In Matthew's genealogy Jesus is listed as having been born of Mary (1) and when he visited his home town of Nazareth, the people wonder how he could be doing such great things since he was only "Mary's son". (2) Later during his ministry when Jesus himself asked his disciples who they thought he was, Peter responded, "You are the Messiah, the Son of the living God." (3) Whose son is Jesus, then, really? One reason Matthew includes the birth story in his Gospel is to answer that question. He wants his readers to understand exactly who the Carpenter of Nazareth actually was.

Son of David

 Matthew begins his Gospel by giving the genealogy of Jesus. Before he begins listing his ancestors, Matthew uses the title "Christ" for Jesus. He actually uses the term as if it were a name. It is used as both a title and a name in the New Testament when referring to Jesus. The word is the Greek form of the Hebrew "Messiah" and means "anointed one". Matthew understood the significance of the title because he follows it by calling Jesus the son of David who was himself the "anointed" king of Israel. In using the term "Christ", Jesus is immediately identified as the Messiah, God's anointed one.

Is it significant or important that Jesus was the Son of David? Matthew's Gospel would be read in churches having both Jewish and Gentile members. (The term "Gentile" refers to all people who are not Jews.) However, he seems to be particularly thinking of Jewish believers as he tells his story. For this audience, the relationship of the Messiah to King David would be very important.

When the first king of Israel, Saul, disobeyed him, God "sought him a man after his own heart." (4) That man was David, the great poet and musician; David, the charismatic warrior who more than any other established the glory of Israel as a nation; David whom God lifted up until "the fame of David went out into all lands; and the Lord brought the fear of him upon all nations" (5) It seems appropriate that the name "David" is given to only one man in the Bible – Israel's greatest king!

Above all, David was devoted to God. He danced with joy as he brought God's ark to Jerusalem and he repented bitterly when the prophet Nathan convicted him of sinning against God. His great poems (Psalms) stand as a tribute to the depth of his personal relationship with God. His great triumphs were God's doing and his kingdom was built on a religious foundation more than a political one.

David the man might have been a worthy human ancestor of the Lord, however, it is as king that David appears in the Messiah's genealogy. It was as king that David sat in his great house and decided that it was not right that God should not also have a house. So he proposed to build God a house. But God said "No!" So you, David, whom I took from "following the sheep to be ruler over my people, over Israel" (6) wish to build me a house. No, David, instead I will build you a house! And what a house it was to be! It would be something more lasting than a house of stone and mortar!

God spoke to David through the prophet Nathan: "Your family shall be established and your kingdom shall stand for all time in my sight, and your throne shall be established forever." (7) For about 400 years, David's descendants would have a political kingdom. But when Babylon carried the Israelites into Exile, God's earthly government came to an end. However, the kingdom did not die in the hearts and expectations of His people. As Jesus began his ministry of healing, "the word went round; Can this be the Son of David?" (8) After the people had seen his deeds and heard his message, they hailed him "Hosanna to the son of David!" (9) as he made his final entrance into Jerusalem. The people had known that it would not be right with Israel until the throne of David was once more established.

Later in his story Matthew will report that the Magi followed the rising star because it was the symbol of the child "born to be king of the Jews." In Luke's Gospel Gabriel described Mary's miracle child to her as one to whom God would give the throne of David and one who would be king over Israel. (10) When Jesus first sent out the twelve apostles, they were to announce that "the kingdom is here". (11) The kingdom had arrived because the throne of David was restored. The Messiah—the anointed one—the King had arrived! The Christ had to be the Son of David because "he will reign over the house of Jacob forever; his kingdom will never end." (12)

In summary, Matthew establishes Jesus as the son of David because God had promised Israel that the throne of David would last forever. The Jewish expectation was of a Messiah who would fulfill that promise. The hope of Israel was for a return to the days of her most glorious king! God's view seems to be that even the most glorious days of an earthly kingdom were at best flawed and fading. (Jesus alludes to the difference between the Messiah and David when He reminds the Jewish teachers of the law that David said in Psalms: God said to my Master, "Sit here at my right hand until I put your enemies under your feet." David here designates the Messiah as 'my Master' — so how can the Messiah also be his 'son'?" (13)

Therefore, the one who would announce to Matthew's generation that the "kingdom of heaven (not the kingdom of David!) was at hand" would be descended from but would be unlike David. David, like his kingdom, was flawed and he too faded. The Messiah, Jesus, would be without flaw and would be eternal. And his kingdom, with its laws written on men's hearts, would be eternal and would consummate in eternal glory!

Son of Abraham

The Old Testament is almost entirely the history of one people. And that history of one people starts with one man—Abraham. No one knows just why God chose Abram, as he was called, to be such a special person. But he was very special. Indeed, God told Abraham to look up into the sky and understand that his descendants would be as countless as the stars. And God had chosen a particular land in which Abraham was to live. With a unique outpouring of grace, Jehovah made wonderful promises to this man! And the promises were marked by an unprecedented covenant which was sealed by God in an ancient ceremony. **Genesis 15** describes a mysterious scene in which a smoking brazier and a flaming torch passed dramatically between the cleaved halves of sacrificed animals. (14) This strange and mystical encounter between God and Abraham marked the beginnings of Israel.

God would tell his people generations later that it was not their special merit that made him choose them as his people. "Know this and don't ever forget it: It's not because of any good that you've done that God is giving you this good land to own. Anything but! You're stubborn as mules." (15) And perhaps Abraham also was not chosen because he had special standing with God. God's inexplicable choice of Abraham seems to have been one of the earliest instances of God's grace. As we learn about Abraham we discover that he was not always perfect before God but as his journey with God progressed his faith seems to grow until it was written of him "and Abram believed in the Lord; and He counted it to him for righteousness." (16)

When God called Abraham to go to a new homeland, which he, God, would show him, he believed God and did as he was told. Apparently Abraham undertook this great journey without question or hesitation. But as Abraham and his wife, Sarah, grew older they continued to be childless even though God had promised to give Abraham descendants countless as the sands of the seashore. Now Abraham believed God would do what he had promised. But he determined to help God keep his word. First he appears to adopt his servant, Eliezer, and assumes he will be his heir. But God reaffirms to him that his original plan is still in place. "Then the word of the LORD came to him: "This man (Eleizer) will not be your heir, but a son coming from your own body will be your heir."" (17)

As more time passed and Sarah continued to be childless, the couple decided it was time once again to help God keep his promise. At Sarah's suggestion Abraham conceived a son with her Egyptian handmaiden, Haggar. (Abraham seems to accept the offer of Haggar from Sarah as fast as Adam accepted the apple from Eve!) But this son, Ishmael, was not the child of God's promise either. Finally God's power overcame the barrenness of Sarah (when she was ninety and her husband 100!) and the heir of God's covenant was born. The miraculous birth of Isaac must have affected Abraham deeply. The child so long awaited and born in the advanced age of his parents was greatly loved.

While Isaac was still just a lad, God gave Abraham what must have been a dismaying and awesome command, "Take your son Isaac, your only son, whom you love, and go to the land of Moriah. There you shall offer him as a sacrifice on one of the hills which I will show you." (18) Abraham reacted in a way which set an eternal standard for faith. Without hinting to Isaac what lie ahead he took him to the appointed place of sacrifice. As the totally trusting father raised the knife over Isaac, the angel of the Lord stayed his hand. "You have not withheld from me your son, your only son." (19)

Until this episode, each time God gave Abraham a command he was told how it would turn out. When he told Abraham to "Go", he also said he would be going to a land "which I will show you." When God told Abraham he would have countless descendants, he explained that this would happen because Sarah would conceive and bear a son. It was when God told Abraham to sacrifice Isaac that he became the supreme example of faith. The Genesis narrative shows Abraham's faith was unwavering even as he led his son up the mountain slopes. As he left his servants with the donkey he told them "Stay here . . . . We will worship and then **WE** will come back to you." (20) Even though God had not told him the outcome of this latest command, Abraham said WE will come back to you. The writer of Hebrews included Abraham in his "Faith Hall of Fame" and said of him: "By faith Abraham, when God tested him, offered Isaac as a sacrifice. He who had received the promises was about to sacrifice his one and only son, even though God had said to him, "It is through Isaac that your offspring will be reckoned." Abraham reasoned that God could raise the dead, and figuratively speaking, he did receive Isaac back from death." (21) Abraham gives us a vivid picture of what it means to fully trust God. Can you go forward in the direction God is calling you, trusting Him, even though you cannot see the outcome?

Later generations of Jewish people would try to appropriate Abraham's righteousness as their own and base their claim to the kingdom of God

on their physical relationship to him. (22) But the apostle Paul, himself
a son of Abraham, saw a new and different relationship. "It is the men of
faith who are Abraham's sons" he writes in Galatians. (23) Paul further
explains that it is through faith that we are also sons of God — in union
with Jesus Christ, distinctions of race, sex and even freedom or slavery
disappear. "But if you belong to Christ, you are the "issue" of Abraham
and so heirs by promise." (24)

Abraham's significance to the Israelites of Old Testament times
was as the father of the nation, the first Israelite as it were. And he was
further revered as the one to whom a special land was to be given and his
descendants would live in that land. As the Messiah arrives, these promises
of the Abrahamic covenant have been fulfilled and their importance has
diminished. Abraham is seen by the New Testament writers in a new light.
He now takes on a new stature as the foremost example of faith; as the
example of faith counting as righteousness. (25) And the Messiah had to be
the son of Abraham because of the third promise God had given Abraham:
" . . . and **all peoples** on earth will be blessed through you." (26)

The fulfillment of this promise is given most famously and elegantly in
the Gospel verse known to all believers: "For God so loved the world that
he gave his one and only Son, that whoever believes in him shall not perish
but have eternal life." (27) Two words in this passage link Abraham and
Jesus. "Whoever" does indeed include "all peoples on earth" and Jesus,
son of Abraham and "one and only Son" of God is the one through whom
the blessing of salvation comes. The second word, "believes", points to
Abraham as the father of us all who have a faith, like his, which can be
counted as righteousness.

Jesus and Abraham, the connection is clear. But it was so from the
beginning. God's promise to Abraham portended a blessing to all nations.
Men of faith from all families of the earth would realize this blessing
through Jesus Christ — Son of Abraham.

QUESTIONS—CHAPTER 1

1. In the Gospels, how many "fathers" of Jesus are mentioned? Why so many?

2. Who is probably the most prominent human "father"?

3. What does "Messiah" mean? Why is it important as a title for Jesus?

4. What great promise did God make to David? Did God keep his promise? How?

5. Both David and Jesus were anointed as kings by God. How does Jesus' kingdom differ from David's kingdom?

6. Why did God choose Abram to be the ancestor of Israel? What term describes God's action?

7. God made a promise to Abram which had three parts. What were they? Has God kept these promises?

8. Abram evidently thought God needed help in fulfilling his promise to give him descendants. How did he try to help God?

9. Why did God wait until Sarah was 90 years old and Abraham was 100 before giving them the promised son?

10. In the Old Testament Abraham is seen as the one who received God's promises which were fulfilled in God's people, Israel. In the New Testament, what new significance does Abraham take on?

REFERENCES

New English Bible, Oxford University Press – Cambridge University Press, 1970 (NEB)

King James Version (KJV)

The Message (MSG)

New International Version (NIV)

The Birth of the Messiah, Raymond E. Brown, Doubleday and Company (1977) ISBN: 0-385-05907-8 (Brown)

All Bible references are NIV unless noted otherwise.

CHAPTER 1

1. Matthew 1:16
2. Mark 6:3
3. Matthew 6:16 NEB)
4. I Samuel 13:14 (KJV)
5. I Chronicles 14:17 (KJV)
6. II Samuel 7:8 (KJV)
7. II Samuel 7:16 (NEB)
8. Matthew 12:23 (NEB)
9. Matthew 21:9 (NEB)
10. Luke 2:32
11. Matthew 10: 7 (MSG)
12. Luke 1:33
13. Luke 20:41-44 (MSG)
14. Genesis 15
15. Deuteronomy 9:5-6 (MSG)
16. Genesis 16:6 (KJV)
17. Genesis 15:4
18. Genesis 22:2 (NEB)
19. Genesis 22:12
20. Genesis 22:5
21. Hebrews 11:17-19
22. Luke 3:8
23. Galatians 3:7 (NEB)
24. Galatians 3:29 (NEB)
25. Romans 4:2
26. Genesis 12:3
27. John 3:16

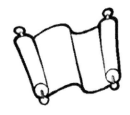

CHAPTER 2

THE FAMILY TREE

"Why waste your money looking up your family tree?
Just go into politics and your opponents will do it for you!"
—*Mark Twain*

Matthew 1:2-17
²Abraham was the father of Isaac,
Isaac the father of Jacob,
Jacob the father of Judah and his brothers,
³Judah the father of Perez and Zerah, whose mother was Tamar,
Perez the father of Hezron,
Hezron the father of Ram,
⁴Ram the father of Amminadab,
Amminadab the father of Nahshon,
Nahshon the father of Salmon,
⁵Salmon the father of Boaz, whose mother was Rahab,
Boaz the father of Obed, whose mother was Ruth,
Obed the father of Jesse,
⁶and Jesse the father of King David.
David was the father of Solomon, whose mother had been Uriah's wife,

⁷Solomon the father of Rehoboam,
Rehoboam the father of Abijah,
Abijah the father of Asa,
⁸Asa the father of Jehoshaphat,

Jehoshaphat the father of Jehoram,
Jehoram the father of Uzziah,
⁹Uzziah the father of Jotham,
Jotham the father of Ahaz,
Ahaz the father of Hezekiah,
¹⁰Hezekiah the father of Manasseh,
Manasseh the father of Amon,
Amon the father of Josiah,
¹¹and Josiah the father of Jeconiah and his brothers at the time of the exile to Babylon.

¹²After the exile to Babylon:
Jeconiah was the father of Shealtiel,
Shealtiel the father of Zerubbabel,
¹³Zerubbabel the father of Abiud,
Abiud the father of Eliakim,
Eliakim the father of Azor,
¹⁴Azor the father of Zadok,
Zadok the father of Akim,
Akim the father of Eliud,
¹⁵Eliud the father of Eleazar,
Eleazar the father of Matthan,
Matthan the father of Jacob,
¹⁶and Jacob the father of Joseph, the husband of Mary, of whom was born Jesus, who is called Christ.
¹⁷Thus there were fourteen generations in all from Abraham to David, fourteen from David to the exile to Babylon, and fourteen from the exile to the Christ.

Genealogies are common in the Bible. It is natural that Matthew follows Old Testament practice and includes a list of Jesus' ancestors in his birth story. However, these lists are full of names difficult to pronounce and they are not often read with much interest. Our modern mind sees little purpose in "going back so far" and consequently we do not understand what is being communicated.

Genealogies were important to Jews for various reasons. It was essential to know to what tribe one belonged because rights, privileges, responsibilities and even homeland were determined by tribal descent. Zechariah, the father of John the Baptist, could serve as a priest in the Jerusalem temple because he was of the tribe of Levi. Luke says Zechariah's wife, Elizabeth, was a descendent of Aaron. (1) When Ezra reestablished the priesthood following the return of the Israelites from exile in Babylon, some men seeking to be priests were excluded as unclean because they could not find their family records. (2) Joseph took Mary to Bethlehem because he "belonged to the house and line of David". (3) Paul attached importance to his being a member of the tribe of Benjamin. (4) When the Jewish historian Josephus wrote his autobiography he started by listing his ancestors which he claims he found in the public records. (5)

In composing his genealogy, Matthew probably had a list on which he based it. It is not possible to know what that list was. It may have included names from Old Testament lists such as found in **Ruth Chapter 4:18-22** and **I Chronicles 1:28, 34 and 2:1-15**. Comparing genealogies from different books in the Bible can be a problem. This is because of such complications as the differences in Greek and Hebrew translations, the fact that kings had regal names which were different from their birth names, and people having only one name. Many times names were very similar causing misunderstandings. Sometimes names were deliberately omitted from genealogies because they were considered unsuitable ("black sheep") and at times grandchildren were considered as "children." Consequently when Luke's genealogy for the Messiah is compared with Matthew's there are notable differences.

It is not the purpose of this study to compare or contrast in detail the two Gospel lists. That can be considered a separate exercise in itself.[1] It has been observed that Biblical genealogies can serve different purposes and consequently do not necessarily always portray precise biological ancestry. (7) For example, Matthew's genealogy presents Jesus as the Hebrew Messiah who fulfills God's promise to David that his kingdom would be eternal while Luke's defines Jesus as the son of Adam, the son of God and thus relates him to all mankind. An important observation to be made regarding Matthew's genealogy is that the Bible records no opposition to Jesus as Messiah on the grounds of his doubtful descent from David.

Some of the names in Matthew's genealogy appear in the Old Testament while others are not found there. Some of the names included

---

[1]   Brown includes a detailed discussion of Matthew's and Luke's genealogies. (6) There are difficulties when the genealogies are considered only as historical records of biological ancestors. His presentation outlines some of the difficulties and includes proposed explanations for them.

by Matthew would probably have special significance to his readers. When Isaac is mentioned in the list, it might remind the reader that Jesus was not descended from the older Ishmael but is Abraham's "son" because of God's direct intervention. In a similar manner Isaac was the father of Jacob and it would be noted that Jesus was not descended from the older Esau but from the younger Jacob, the one chosen by God. (8) When he writes "**Jacob the father of Judah and his brothers**," he emphasizes that Judah was selected from among **"his brothers"** in accordance with the prophetic passage in Genesis which states that Judah will be given the eternal scepter. (9) Matthew wants the reader to realize that God has been working throughout Israel's history to bring about the present moment, the birth of the Messiah. He will emphasize this again at the conclusion of this section.

Probably the most interesting and unusual aspect of Matthew's genealogy is his inclusion of women. It was not the Jewish custom to include women in a list of ancestors. What is Matthew's purpose or message in doing this? Much has been speculated and theories abound. In considering the question, it helps to know the women mentioned.

Tamar is listed as the mother of the twins, Perez and Zerah. She was the daughter-in-law of Judah, the one son among Israel's twelve sons who was chosen to be special. Tamar had been the Canaanite wife of Judah's oldest son, Er. When Er died leaving her alone, the law required that the deceased man's brother, Onan, should marry his widow and thus perpetuate his brother's name. (10) However, Onan refused to marry Tamar and Judah also withheld his third son, Shilah, beyond the promised time. Having run out of patience, Tamar offered herself, disguised as a prostitute, to Judah. He did not recognize her and the result of their union was the birth of twins.

The Rahab listed has been understood to mean the prostitute who lived in Jericho, although her place in the genealogy is not consistent with when she appears in the Old Testament. (11) Joshua led the Israelites across the Jordan River and into the Promised Land. To prepare for the attack on Jericho, he sent two men to spy out the city. They stayed in Rahab's house. When the king of Jericho heard about the visitors, he sent men to Rahab's house and demanded that she produce the spies. Instead she hid the men in stalks of flax on the roof of her house and sent the king's men on a false trail. She then told the spies that she had heard about the mighty deeds of Yahweh and she knew Yahweh to be "God in heaven above and on earth below." (12) She helped the men escape down a rope from a window of her house which was built into the wall of the city. She tied a scarlet thread in the window of her house to identify it and when the Israelites later destroyed Jericho, she and her family were saved and settled with the Israelites. Matthew lists her as the mother of Boaz, the great grandfather of King David.

Ruth was a Moabite woman and she had married a Hebrew from Bethlehem who was living in Moab. When her husband died, she chose to go with her mother-in-law, Naomi, back to Bethlehem rather than remain with her own people. This was particularly remarkable since Moabites had been one of Israel's most hated enemies. In **Deuteronomy 23:3** the command was given that "no Ammonite or Moabite or any of his descendants may enter the assembly of the Lord, even down to the tenth generation." Ruth's expression of affection for Naomi spawned a poignant modern love song. "Whither thou. goest, I will go; and where thou lodgest, I will lodge; thy people shall be my people, and thy God, my God." (13) In Bethlehem she met and became the wife of Boaz, the kinsman of her husband. Their son would become the grandfather of David.

The wife of Uriah was Bathsheba. She must have been very beautiful. When King David saw her bathing from the roof of his palace, he immediately summoned her to his bed. She subsequently conceived a child with David as the father. David wanted to have Bathsheba for his wife so he arranged for her husband to be killed in battle. (14) It was probably David's worst episode and the prophet, Nathan, deeply convicted him of his sin in a touching parable. (15) Bathsheba eventually became the mother of Solomon.

Why do women, and especially *these* women, appear in a Biblical literary form normally reserved for only men? Any explanation is, of course, based on speculation. Several have been proposed. Three of the women were definitely sinners (but aren't we all!). The fourth, Ruth, seems more pious. However, the quaint description of her rendezvous with Boaz at the threshing floor may depict less than innocent goings-on. As a Moabite, her standing with the Israelites would be very low. If these women are meant to stand out as particular sinners, then their association with Jesus emphasizes his role as the savior of sinners.

Another possible reason for listing the four is that they were probably all foreigners, that is, they were not Israelites. Rahab and Ruth were certainly not Jewish and Matthew describes Bathsheba as the wife of Uriah. Since Uriah was a Hittite, this designation appears to highlight Bathsheba's probable ancestry. The pre-Christian "Book of Jubilees" calls

Tamar an Aramean (16) which would make her a Canaanite. Matthew's Gospel seems to be directed to a Jewish audience. But there would have been many Gentiles in the churches of his day and Matthew may have wanted all his readers, especially the Jewish ones, to understand that salvation for Gentiles was always part of God's plan. Thus Matthew, by including Gentiles in the genealogy of Jesus, shows that the Jewish Messiah is linked to all nations, echoing the first promise to Abraham.

Maybe Matthew is simply elevating woman to a new relationship with God that was missing before. There were prominent women in Israel's history but women were generally overshadowed in the patriarchal culture of Old Testament times. In the birth story Matthew anticipates themes which will appear as the Gospel story unfolds. Thus, Jesus is constantly reaching out to and touching the lives of women during his ministry. He seems to have been especially close to Mary and Martha. And there was a widow in Nain for whom Jesus had restored her only son who had died, (17) the woman who suffered from bleeding for 12 years and only wanted to touch his cloak (18) and the prostitute who washed his feet with her tears and wiped them with her hair (19) to mention only a few. And as Paul states it so plainly "There is no such thing as Jew or Greek, slave and freeman, *male and female*; for you are all one person in Christ Jesus." (20)

Still another common aspect of these women was the scandal associated with them. Each had impropriety, or at least its appearance, in their unions or their backgrounds. From prostitute to Moabite, their characters were blemished. Nevertheless, God used them for a special purpose. What may have appeared as irregular or even sinful could be understood as calling forth the Holy Spirit's intervention in the flow of events. Even imperfect individuals can be used by God for his perfect purposes. What seems to be evil can be used by God for good—for his purpose. Long ago another Joseph told his brothers "You intended to harm me, but God intended it for good to accomplish what is now being done, the saving of many lives." (21)

Now in the eyes of many, another "scandal" had been unfolded. Mary had become pregnant although she had never been with her lawful husband. The assumption was that she had been unfaithful to Joseph. But, as Matthew would explain, it was actually God at work again!

The genealogy closes with a hint of what is to follow. The orderly language of the listing is interrupted by a significant change in wording at the climax. Matthew is quite clear, Joseph was not the father of Jesus;

he was the husband of Mary. And Mary was the one who gave birth to Jesus called Messiah. Luke later describes Joseph as the man who people thought (or supposed) to be the Father of Jesus. (22) Matthew will subsequently go on to explain this!

Matthew pauses before beginning his explanation of Jesus' birth to put the event into proper Jewish perspective in verse 17. The first section of the genealogy covers the time between Abraham and David and can be designated the "pre-monarchical" section. In this section, as seen above, there are allusions to God actively selecting or choosing those who would be in the line leading to "King David". The section closes by using this term, "King", for the only time in the genealogy.

In the next "monarchical" section, from Solomon to Jeconiah, Matthew lists the kings who were descended from David and who ruled from Jerusalem. It concludes with "the exile to Babylon".

In the midst of his list of names, Matthew inserts into his genealogy the exile of Israel to Babylon. In the period from Abraham to David, Israel is established as a nation of God's people by the divinely orchestrated events of the Exodus. It is a period of ascendancy for the descendants of Abraham. In David and Solomon's time, Israel reached the peak of its glory and power. But as the people, led by their kings, turned from Jehovah a period of descent set in. The Exile to Babylon became the low point. "By the rivers of Babylon we sat and wept when we remembered Zion." and "How can we sing the songs of the LORD while in a foreign land?" (23)

It was also to be a significant pivot point for the nation. Ripped from their "promised land" and, more importantly, from the center of worship, the Temple, the people's dedication to Yahweh was severely threatened. While many of the Jews were doubtless absorbed into the Babylonian culture, others in significant numbers must have vigorously preserved their religious traditions. Their Mosaic faith seems to have been strengthened by the captivity experience. If God could no longer be accessed in the Jerusalem temple, he could be found through prayer. [12]Then you will call upon me and come and pray to me, and I will listen to you. [13]You will seek me and find me when you seek me with all your heart. [14]I will be found by you," declares the LORD, "and will bring you back from captivity. I will gather you from all the nations and places where I have banished you," declares the LORD, "and will bring you back to the place from which I carried you into exile." (24) With the return from

Exile, a new period of ascendancy was begun and it would climax in the birth of the promised Messiah.

In the third and last section, "after the exile to Babylon" to "Jesus, who is called Christ," the coming of the Messiah is given equality, or more correctly, climatic superiority over two other great events in Israel's history; the rise of Israel's greatest king and the exile to Babylon which had changed the nation.

Matthew states that Abraham and David are 14 generations apart. And there are 14 generations from David to the Exile. Messiah's coming was another 14 generations from Israel's pivotal crisis, the Babylonian captivity. The event of Jesus' birth is given special importance by placing it last in the final set of 14. In the Hebrew language each letter was given a number and the letters spelling David's name had the numeric equivalent of 14! This may have influenced Matthew's allusion to this number in Jehovah's time table for His Messianic plan and he saw a symmetry in the ancestors of Jesus which demonstrated that plan.

A careful count of the actual generations listed seems to result in 13 instead of 14 for the first and third sections. If Matthew is counting Abraham's generation in the first section that would make 14. It has also been suggested that if David is counted in both the first and second sections, the mathematics improves. (25) In the third section, there may have been confusion between the names of two kings: *Jechoniah* and *Jehoiakim*. A copyist error may have been caused by the similarity of the names. Since *Jehoiakim* was the father of *Jechoniah* (Jehoiachin), a generation may have been inadvertently skipped in the scriptural transmission process.[2]

Also, Matthew's lists do not appear complete when compared to **II Chronicles 3**. Further explanations for this and the possibly forced symmetry built around the number 14 are possible. (See above footnote 1) However, Matthew's message, which is the important consideration, is clear enough. God has worked in history in an intentional and even orderly way. The Messiah has arrived according to God's plan. And that arrival is positioned relative to the other great events in Israel's history in such a way that its significance is unmistaken.

---

2   Confusion is not limited to copyists of the ancient world! A comparison of just
     three New Testament translations shows the NIV using Jeconiah in 1:12, the KJV
     goes with Jechonias and the MSG likes Jehoichin!

QUESTIONS—CHAPTER 2

1. What is particularly unusual about Matthew's genealogy?

2. What do the women mentioned in the genealogy share in common? What might be significant about what they have in common?

3. Which of Jacob's 12 sons is given special honor?

4. If Matthew had wanted to avoid reminding his readers of the most shameful episode of David's career, he would not have mentioned what character in the genealogy?

5. What character in the genealogy pretended to be a prostitute and why? Was she justified in doing this?

6. In addition to the people listed in the genealogy what event is mentioned and why?

7. What use of the number 14 does Matthew make in the genealogy? What is his purpose?

8. Every male in the genealogy is said to be "the father of . . ." except one? Who was that and why the change in language?

9. When comparing genealogies from different sources, what particular perspective is important to remember?

REFERENCES

New English Bible, Oxford University Press – Cambridge University Press, 1970 (NEB)

King James Version (KJV)

The Message (MSG)

New International Version (NIV)

The Birth of the Messiah, Raymond E. Brown, Doubleday and Company (1977) ISBN: 0-385-05907-8 (Brown)

The Peoples New Testament with Notes, B. W. Johnson, Gospel Advocate Company (Johnson)

The Daily Study Bible Series, William Barclay, Revised Edition Copyright 1975, The Westminster Press (Barclay)

All Bible references are NIV unless noted otherwise.

CHAPTER 2

1. Luke 1:5
2. Ezra 2:62
3. Luke 2:4
4. Philippians 3:5
5. Barclay Volume 1 Page 12
6. Brown Page 64-94
7. Brown Page 65
8. Genesis 27
9. Genesis 49:10
10. Deuteronomy 25:5-10
11. Joshua 2:1-21
12. Joshua 2:11 NEB
13. Ruth 1:16 KJV
14. II Samuel 11
15. II Samuel 12:1ff
16. Brown Page 72
17. Luke 7:11
18. Matthew 9:20
19. Luke 7:37
20. Galatians 3:28 NEB
21. Genesis 50:20
22. Luke 3:23
23. Psalms 137:1,6
24. Jeremiah 29:12-14
25 Johnson Volume 1 Page 20

CHAPTER 3

THE INSIDE STORY

The doctor smiled at the young lady sitting across from him. "I have good news for you. You are going to have a baby!" he said. She was shocked. "That can't possibly be true!" she exclaimed. "It is simply impossible!" The doctor rose and walked across the room and began to stare out the window. "What are you doing?" his patient asked. "The last time this happened a bright star rose in the east. I am just looking to see if that star is returning!"

Matthew 1:18-20 [18]This is how the birth of Jesus Christ came about: His mother Mary was pledged to be married to Joseph, but before they came together, she was found to be with child through the Holy Spirit. [19]Because Joseph her husband was a righteous man and did not want to expose her to public disgrace, he had in mind to divorce her quietly. [20]But after he had considered this, an angel of the Lord appeared to him in a dream and said, "Joseph son of David, do not be afraid to take Mary home as your wife, because what is conceived in her is from the Holy Spirit.

Starting with verse 18 of the first chapter Matthew begins his actual birth story. He writes that he is now going to explain how the birth of Jesus Christ happened or "came about." Matthew is now going to give his readers the inside story. Here is the truth of what happened.

Joseph is the major character in Matthew's narrative. He is centrally involved in the action and receives divine announcements and communications from angels and in visions. Perhaps this is consistent with the patriarchal emphasis in Israel's history. On the other hand, Luke presents the birth story from Mary's perspective. While Matthew and Luke are synoptic Gospels (meaning seen with the same eyes), the birth story is viewed from distinctly different angles by these two Gospel writers. In our study we are considering only Matthew's story.

There had obviously been questions about Mary's pregnancy and the circumstances of her son's birth. The rumor that Mary had become pregnant before she was married probably had attached scandal to Jesus' birth. In the anti-Christian writing of Celsus of the second century A.D. a Roman soldier named Panthera is identified as the father of an illegitimate Jesus. (1) Tertullian writing in ca. A.D. 197 mentions that one of the defaming charges against Jesus was that he was the son of a prostitute. (1) In subsequent centuries his enemies continued to dismiss Jesus with this charge of illegitimacy. The New Testament hints that there may have been stories about Jesus having a disreputable background in his lifetime. In **Chapter 8 of the Gospel of John**, Jesus challenges the claim of his Jewish opponents that they are descendants of Abraham since their deeds are not worthy of Abraham. They reply in verse 41 "We are not illegitimate children." Is the unstated "Like you are!" implied here? The timing of the birth of Jesus relative to the marriage of Joseph and Mary may have given his enemies a basis to charge "scandal!" That may be another reason Matthew wanted to explain what had really occurred.

But Matthew's careful explanation is not just to correct mistaken impressions about Jesus' ancestry. The telling of the Messiah's true birth story would reveal much about exactly who Jesus was (and is!).

And the true story was too good to keep! An experienced mystery writer would have postponed the most crucial fact until the proper suspense had been orchestrated! But Matthew blurts out the astounding revelation in the very first verse of his story (verse 18). Mary is with child *by the Holy Spirit!* Or as the Message Version puts it "It was by the Holy Spirit. But he (Joseph) didn't know that." From the very first Matthew puts the reader on notice—this is no ordinary nativity story. And the birth of Jesus is certainly not one besmirched with scandal. To make matters clear, Matthew continues to fill in the details.

"Mary was pledged to be married to Joseph." What does this mean? Were Mary and Joseph married at the time of Jesus' conception? The answer is "yes" and "no"! Mary's status as the "wife" of Joseph must be understood in the context of the prevailing customs. According to these Jewish customs, "pledged" (or betrothed), from a legal standpoint, was equivalent to marriage. In the first step of the two-part marriage procedure, a verbal declaration was made to the prospective bride. This was accompanied by a small gift and was given in the presence of two witnesses. The betrothal could also come about by delivering a written declaration to the bride-to-be. This formal exchange of consent was usually entered into when the girl was 12 to 13 years old. From this time forward the couple was considered to be formally married.

However, the "wife" continued to live apart from her "husband" in her father's house. The betrothal period typically lasted about one year in the case of a virgin and she could be released from the marriage contract only by a letter of divorce. During this period the "wife" was subject to the law's penalty for adultery if that should occur. At the end of the betrothal the second step came when the groom (or husband) took his wife to his family home and the marriage relationship was completed. (The parable in **Chapter 25 of Matthew** tells of a bridegroom who is late in coming home.)

It was apparently during the time after their marriage contract was arranged and before they began living together as husband and wife that Mary was found to be pregnant. What a dilemma for any man! But it was particularly difficult for Joseph. And Matthew tells us why. Joseph was a righteous man. The word "righteous" can also mean "just." The New English Bible uses the phrase "a man of principle" to describe Joseph.

The whole matter was similar to a situation presented to Jesus later in his ministry. A woman caught as an adulteress was brought before the Lord as a test by his enemies. (2) What to do? The law was very clear as the Pharisees were quick to point out. The penalty prescribed for adultery was death. (3). What does a just man, a righteous man, do when confronted with the seemingly conflicting demands of the law on one hand and the demands of mercy on the other? Jesus confounded the accusers by forcing them to look at themselves. The law required the witnesses to throw the first stones (4) but Jesus added a "qualifier": "If any one of you *is without sin*, let him be the first to throw a stone at her." Apparently none felt qualified! The accusers melted away and Jesus was left alone with the frightened woman. He sent her away with the admonition to sin no more.

There were no obvious accusers in Joseph's situation nor was adultery actually present except perhaps in Joseph's mind. So Joseph's situation was different. Matthew wants us (and particularly his fellow Jews) to understand that Joseph respected and lived by the law. The "father" of Jesus was not an unbelieving Jew or one who was on the fringes of God's special community. Since he was a just man who followed the law, he could not possibly take Mary as his wife. **Deuteronomy 22:20-21** But Joseph was also a good man. He was "unwilling to put her to shame." So he resolved to obey the law in a loving manner. He would set aside the marriage contract but it would be done quietly.

Perhaps Joseph's attitude and plan to resolve his predicament should be a model for modern Christians. Often in today's world we hear harsh rhetoric and see unloving conduct supposedly in defense of God's laws. Jesus' enemies spoke out against him for "doing what is unlawful" when his disciples picked grain to eat on the Sabbath. (5) Jesus response was "The Sabbath was made for man, not man for the Sabbath." The implication seems to be that God's laws are intended to bless us, not harm us. When we bludgeon one another with God's commandments (as we understand them!), we are surely missing the mark. Joseph did not set aside the law but found a way to honor it in a loving manner. Perhaps he had in mind one of the most striking passages from the holy scrolls he would have seen unrolled each Sabbath. A passage which would be a welcome addition to the refrigerator doors in our homes today:

> He has showed you, O man, what is good.
> And what does the LORD require of you?
> To act **justly** *and* to love **mercy**
> and to walk humbly with your God **Micah 6:8**

But Joseph's plans to gently divorce his intended bride were interrupted. An angel of the Lord visited him in a dream. The angel addresses Joseph as "Son of David". This is the only occasion in the New Testament in which this title is applied to anyone other than Jesus. It again emphasizes Joseph's (and Jesus') descent from Israel's greatest king. Matthew is very clear on this and it can be noted that Jesus' claim to Messiahship was never challenged for lack of Davidic descent.

Joseph's visitor told him "do not be afraid" and this "angel of the Lord" will next appear in Matthew's Gospel **(Chapter 28)** at the empty tomb where he repeats this admonition. He announces to the two Marys when they come looking for Jesus' body, "He is risen". But first he says to the two women, just as he did to Joseph, "Do not be afraid". Later, the women encounter Jesus himself and he greets them and then says, "Do not be afraid." This pattern is repeated in Luke's Gospel. When the angel appears to Zechariah in the temple to tell him his and his wife's prayers for a son will be answered, he first says "Do not be afraid." (6) When Mary was troubled by Gabriel's appearance, he tells her "Do not be afraid." (7) When the angel of the Lord appeared to the shepherds in the fields outside Bethlehem to tell them a Savior had been born in a stable, he first had to ease their fears; "Do not be afraid," the angel said. (8) In each of these divine-human encounters the Godly message is that something extraordinary is happening and you are part of it. Don't fear that!

In the context of the angel speaking to Joseph, "Do not be afraid" seems to mean don't fear breaking the law by taking Mary into your household for she is not an adulteress. But it could also include don't fear being confronted by Jehovah and being part of His plan. When God Almighty enters his created world, it is apparent that fear or awe comes upon those who are present when God's messenger speaks to them! It is as if God is saying you are right to fear the one who spoke the heavens and earth into existence and has "the whole world in his hands". But I come as one who loves you and my message is one of great joy and blessing. Matthew's first chapter and his last chapter both say it: "Do not be afraid."

The angel is quick to tell Joseph, "son of David", that although the child Mary is carrying will be a descendant of David in a legal sense, his conception did not involve him or any other man. Mary will deliver the baby Jesus just as all mothers deliver their babies. But the angel gives Joseph the startling news that this baby was *conceived* by the power of the Holy Spirit. (Thus, it is more correct to speak of a virgin conception than a virgin birth.) It is important to note that Jesus' conception is never portrayed as a sexual union between a "god" and a human female. This type of "divine"-human mating is a prominent feature of mythical tales of gods visiting earth but is never associated with Jehovah God! The Holy Spirit is acting as God's creative agent. It reminds us of the world's creation as presented in **Genesis 1**: "In the beginning God created the heavens and the earth. Now the earth was formless and empty, darkness was over the surface of the deep, and the **Spirit of God** was hovering over the waters." The Spirit was God's creative agent! For this reason, because her pregnancy resulted from God's creative action, Joseph is told to "take Mary home as your wife."

The Bible records other unusual births. In the **first Chapter of I Samuel**, Elkanah is described as a man who had two wives. One had children, but of Hannah whom he loved it was said "the LORD had closed her womb". Hannah was so distraught that she begged God to relieve her misery by giving her a son and promised to give that son to the Lord for all of his life. The Lord blessed her by giving her Samuel, the great prophet, as her son. Samuel's birth received divine assistance, but he had a human father. Similar circumstances attended the birth of John the Baptist. His parents, Zachariah and Elizabeth, "lived honorably before God" but had no children because Elizabeth was barren. Even though the couple was past the age of bearing children, the Lord intervened and John was born to them. But his father was Zechariah. And, of course, Abraham and Sarah became parents by God's special intervention long after giving up hope of ever having a child. These births were unusual, even miraculous, but in each case a human father was necessary.

But Jesus is unique and the Gospel writers are clear in their portrayal of this uniqueness. By the time Mark wrote his Gospel Jesus would have been thought by many to be the son of Joseph the carpenter who lived in Nazareth. But Mark begins his story by declaring it to be the "Gospel of Jesus Christ *the Son of God*." When Jesus makes his first appearance a few verses later, it is to be baptized by John. As Jesus came out of the water "a voice came from heaven. You are my son." (9) Luke describes how John came to be born to Zechariah and Elizabeth in spite of her being barren for many years. He then contrasts John's birth with the totally unique birth of Jesus. Luke relates how Mary is explicitly told that the child she is to conceive will be the result of the power of the Holy Spirit coming over her. For that reason the child will be known as the *Son of God*. (10) In John's Gospel the writer simply says that the Word was God, and the Word was with God and through the Word all things came to be. And Jesus was that Word. (11)

When Matthew reports the angel's assertion that Mary's child is by the Holy Spirit, he means that God is acting directly in mankind's existence. The child will be his Son in a very direct and real way. In stating that Jesus is to be born of a virgin by the direct action of God, Matthew is emphasizing that he is totally different. He is not just a great prophet as was Samuel. He is not just an eagerly awaited son who would bless his people as was Isaac. He is not just a great messenger from God proclaiming repentance as was John the Baptist. Although Jesus was to fulfill all of these roles in his ministry, he was so much more.

Brown puts it this way: "Even if the intervention of God through the Holy Spirit had been required many times in the long genealogical record of the Messiah, His intervention through the Spirit in the conception and birth of Jesus is not just one more in a series. Jesus is the final and once-for-all manifestation of God's presence with us, which is so much the work of the Spirit that for the first time in the genealogical record of the Messiah no human begetter can be listed." (12)

QUESTIONS—CHAPTER 3

1. Were Joseph and Mary married when Mary became pregnant? Would it have been considered a "scandal" for Mary to be pregnant at this time?

2. Why did Joseph believe he could not go through with his planned marriage to Mary?

3. Is the "modern" view of adultery different than Joseph's?

4. What "unusual" births are described in the Bible? Was the birth of Jesus "unusual"?

5. When Joseph is addressed by an angel in a dream, how does the angel address Joseph? Why is this important?

6. Why was Joseph's conduct when he learned that Mary was going to have a child important to Matthew's overall Gospel presentation?

7. Who is God's agent for creation?

8. Some have said the virgin birth (conception) of Jesus is not a believable story and does nothing to enhance his stature. What do you think?

REFERENCES

New English Bible, Oxford University Press – Cambridge University Press, 1970 (NEB)

King James Version (KJV)

The Message (MSG)

New International Version (NIV)

The Birth of the Messiah, Raymond E. Brown, Doubleday and Company (1977) ISBN: 0-385-05907-8 (Brown)

All Bible references are NIV unless noted otherwise.

CHAPTER 3

1. Brown Appendix V page 535
2. John 8:3ff
3. Leviticus 20:10
4. Deuteronomy 17:5-7
5. Mark 2:24-27
6. Luke 1:13
7. Luke 1:30
8. Luke 2:10
9. Mark1:11
10. Luke 1:35
11. John 1:1
12. Brown page 153

CHAPTER 4

WHAT'S IN A NAME?

"A good name is more desirable than great riches; to be esteemed is better than silver or gold."

Proverbs 22:1 (NIV)

Matthew 1:21-25 ²¹**She will give birth to a son, and you are to give him the name Jesus, because he will save his people from their sins."**²²**All this took place to fulfill what the Lord had said through the prophet:** ²³**"The virgin will be with child and will give birth to a son, and they will call him Immanuel"—which means, "God with us."**²⁴**When Joseph woke up, he did what the angel of the Lord had commanded him and took Mary home as his wife.** ²⁵**But he had no union with her until she gave birth to a son. And he gave him the name Jesus.**

As Matthew continues his story in verse 21 of the first chapter the angel explains the most important aspect of the coming child's existence. In typically Jewish fashion he discloses the name which is to be given the son Mary will bear. In our modern times names are often chosen whimsically. A certain name sounds good or happens to be popular at the time. A name is taken from a current hero or a beloved ancestor. In the stories from the Bible, names were much more significant.

In **Genesis Chapter 12** God made a promise to Abram: "I will bless those who bless you, and whoever curses you I will curse; and **all peoples on earth will be blessed through you**." (1) That name, Abram, means "exalted father" and seems appropriate for the man receiving such a promise. (In Jesus time this man would be called "Father" by the Jews.

For example, in John's Gospel the opponents of Jesus asked him "Are you greater than our father Abraham?") (2) God is determined on his plan and wants to make sure Abram understands his determination. We see in **Genesis Chapter 15** that God establishes a special covenant with Abram in a solemn ceremony in which he promises to give him countless descendants. In **Chapter 17** God confirms that covenant. "Abram fell face down, and God said to him "As for me, this is my covenant with you: You will be the father of many nations."" (3) To mark his words and establish them for all time, God changes Abram's name: "No longer will you be called Abram; your name will be Abraham, for I have made you a father of many nations. "Exalted father" becomes "father of many". His name explains who Abraham is!

It is striking that God says "I **have made** you a father of many nations." When God makes this statement to Abraham, he is ninety-nine years old, his wife Sarah almost ninety and they have had no children! God is so sure of His plan that he speaks of a seeming impossibility as if it has already occurred. Do we today understand God's promises as being so sure that they can be considered as already fulfilled? The new name becomes the very embodiment of God's covenant promise.

Isaac was given his name meaning "he laughed" which denoted the reaction his father Abraham had when God told him he would have a son at 100 years of age! (4) Jacob's name signified that he had supplanted his older, twin brother, Esau, in securing their father's blessing. (5) When he wrestled with an angel, his name was changed to Israel because "you have struggled with God and with men and have overcome." (6) Throughout the pages of Jewish history names often communicated essential information about the people who bore them.

We can further understand the significance of a name in Bible stories when reading about Moses' burning bush experience. When he was commissioned by God to lead Israel out of Egypt, Moses asked God whom he should tell the Israelites had sent him. (7) He was seeking more than just a name to drop in future conversations with Pharaoh. As we have seen a name often expressed the essential nature of an individual and conveyed the character of the one bearing it. God's answer, to Moses, "I am who I am" is enigmatic at best. It seems as if God is saying that there is no "name" that conveys adequately my essence or nature. Nevertheless Moses is apparently trying to discover whatever he can about God by learning His name. (The latest telescopes can apparently see across a universe that is more than 30 billion light years across; a light year being the distance covered by light traveling 186,000 miles per second! And that is not necessarily the size of the universe—just how far we can see with today's technology and it sounds like an "eternal" distance! It is not surprising that the One who created such a universe cannot be named or described in easily understood or precise terms!)

Since in Jewish history names were often very important, it is not surprising that one of the things the angel told Joseph about Mary's child was his name. It was to be Jesus, Savior, "for he will save his people from their sins." The Hebrew form of "Jesus" is Joshua or Yehoshuah meaning "Yahweh is salvation" or "Yahweh saves". The best known "Joshua" before "Jesus of Nazareth" was the successor to Moses. He was the one who led the Israelites into the Promised Land with the conquest of Canaan.

When it came time for Abraham's descendants to cross the Jordan River into the land flowing with milk and honey, God raised up a skilled leader and courageous warrior. There were battles to be fought, cities to be taken and obstacles to be overcome. Joshua was there to lead the people. But the Promised Land they possessed was an earthly one. It subsequently slipped from their grasp and is being fought over to this day. It was a Promised Land which, as with all earthly kingdoms, would not endure. There were indeed glorious times which reached their peak during David's reign. But eventually enemies came, conquered Jerusalem, destroyed the temple and carried the people away to captivity.

In the **eleventh Chapter of Hebrews**, the writer praises the great ones in Israel's history who lived by faith. They did not see the fulfillment of God's ultimate promise but the writer says "like the faithful ones of old, we long "for a better country, the heavenly one."" (8) Whether this world is a glorious sojourn for us or a struggling one, it is not our home. We are just passing through! While his namesake led the Israelites into a temporary Promised Land, Jesus points the way to an eternal home. He would tell His disciples "I am the Way, . . . no one comes to the Father (in Heaven) except by me." (9)

Jesus was given his name because salvation was his chief business. Many have said that the sayings of Jesus, particularly his Sermon on the Mount, constitute man's highest moral code and these sayings are the very core of Christianity. Mahatma Gandhi said, "The message of Jesus is contained in the Sermon on the Mount, unadulterated and taken as a whole." (10). These views of Jesus are entirely wrong!

We should give our full attention to live out his sayings in our lives because they are divine instructions coming from divine wisdom. They lead to mankind's highest good in this life. But Jesus' main purpose for coming into our world was not to give good advice on how to live. His main purpose was not to give us a code of conduct which would qualify us for His Kingdom. Rather his unique personage, Son of God, meant His death on the cross opened the door to salvation to those who accepted not just his sayings, but who accepted him! Jesus confirmed his name and his mission when he said, "For the Son of Man came to seek and to **save** what was lost." (11) There are others who were given the name Jesus and some are mentioned in the Bible. (12) However, it seems that Mary's child *must* have that name! "For there is no other name under heaven given among men whereby we must be saved." (13) Matthew's birth story declares the mission of Jesus by identifying the name he must have and why. He would save lost people!

In verse 22 Matthew makes the first of several Old Testament citations—"all this happened in order to fulfill . . ." The use of these citations strongly suggests that Matthew has Jewish readers in mind. Jewish Christians were struggling with non-believing Jews when Matthew wrote his Gospel. He was giving them assurance that their Messiah and Savior did not repudiate their Jewish heritage but actually fulfilled Old Testament prophecy. Israel's prophets had spoken often of the coming Messiah. Any messianic claim would have to reflect Jewish expectations. Jesus would say "Do not think that I have come to abolish the Law or the Prophets; I have not come to abolish them but to fulfill them. (14) Consequently, Matthew explains in his birth story and elsewhere in his Gospel that God is keeping his promises to his people.

The Gospel writer says that the miraculous way Mary's child was conceived was to fulfill a prophecy given in **Isaiah 7:14**. This assertion has caused controversy for hundreds of years (in the *second century* a Jewish scholar debated the well known Christian, Justin, on the meaning of this passage) and has been discussed elsewhere by others. (15) Disagreements center on the word frequently translated "virgin". The Hebrew Bible uses a Hebrew word more correctly translated "young girl," however in the cultural setting of Isaiah it would be essentially synonymous with virgin. The Septuagint Greek Old Testament uses the equivalent of "virgin" and this text is probably Matthew's reference.

To understand Matthew's purpose in quoting Isaiah we must understand prophecy. Prophecy in the Bible is chiefly God's instruction and warning to the hearers (Israel). At times it also includes God's vision of distant future events. In some cases it seems to include admonitions for the present and prophecies for future expectations at the same time. It has been proposed that Old Testament prophecy can be thought of as sometimes "predication with verification" and sometimes "beginning and completion." (16)

In **Isaiah 7:14** the prophet gave a sign to King Ahaz.[3] "The virgin (or young girl) will be with child and will give birth to a son, and will call him Immanuel." That girl lived and that son was born in the king's life time. The birth was to be God's sign to King Ahaz that God would be with his people in this time of distress. The birth of the child in God's timing, not the miraculous nature of its conception, was the sign to Ahaz.

When God cursed the serpent in the Garden of Eden, he "put enmity between you (the snake) and the woman, between your seed and her seed; He shall bruise you on the head, and you shall bruise him on the heel." (17). There has generally been "enmity" between men (women included!) and snakes ever since. However, in a deeper spiritual sense this passage has been understood to foretell the battle between the Messiah and Satan that would climax at Calvary.

In a similar way Matthew sees Isaiah's prophecy in a Christological light that goes beyond its original meaning to King Ahaz and his contemporaries. In *verse 13* King Ahaz is addressed as "the House of David". Attention is thus drawn once again to the Davidic lineage of Mary's child. Matthew further sees God's choice of "the" virgin and the prediction of a child born to her in verse 14 as pointing to the miraculous conception of the Messiah hundreds of years later. This link helps explains God's action in bringing His Son into the world. "The birth of Jesus Christ happened like this" all according to God's pre-announced plan.

---

[3]   The Aramean King Rezin of Damacus (Syria) and King Pekah of Israel (Ephrain: the Northern Kingdom) were organizing a revolt against Assyria, the "superpower." When King Ahaz of Judah refused to join the revolt, they turned on him, surrounded Jerusalem, and plotted to put a vassal on the throne of Judah. To save himself, Ahaz planned to appeal for aid to King Tiglath-Pileser of Assyria; but Isaiah opposed this, knowing that while the Assyrians would destroy Judah's enemies, they would also reduce Judah to vassalage. Isaiah urged Ahaz to have faith in Yahweh's power to deliver Jerusalem and Judah, and he offered the king a sign from Yahweh. When the king refused, Isaiah angrily proclaimed that a sign would still be given to him - the sign of **Isaiah 7:14**. - "The Birth of the Messiah", Raymond Brown P. 147

The child's title, from the prophet's mouth, was Immanuel, "God with us". God had been with his people in various ways throughout Israel's history. He had appeared as a cloud, as fire, as a bright light, as a still small voice and as a thunderclap. Now, in the most personal and intimate way, God would reveal himself in human form as he moved among his people from birth to death. Matthew's inclusion of the title "Immanuel" calls attention to the "with you" aspect of Jesus' ministry and he concludes his Gospel with the same emphasis by quoting Jesus: "And be assured, I am *with you* always, to the end of time." (18)

Joseph awoke from his remarkable dream fully persuaded as to what he should do. His action may seem unremarkable to us but it is significant to Matthew. Joseph does what a just, upright Jew would be expected to do under the circumstances. He obeys! When he takes Mary as his wife and gives the child the name directed by the angel, he accepts Jesus as his "son" and becomes his "father". Thus, the Messiah is "adopted" into the house of David and becomes the son of David in fulfillment of God's promise to his people. In the Chapter 1 genealogy, Matthew showed that Jesus was the descendant of David but was not begotten of Joseph. He has now explained how that was accomplished. (When Matthew writes "But he (Joseph) had no union with her until she gave birth to a son", he is again emphasizing that Joseph had no part in the conception of her baby.)

Equally important in this passage is the affirmation to believing Jews who would be reading Matthew's Gospel in the first century Christian churches. They have not abandoned their "Jewishness" by obediently accepting Jesus—they are following the example of the "upright" Jew who had become the earthly father of the Messiah!

QUESTIONS—CHAPTER 4

1. Why did God change "the first Israelite's" name?

2. What significance do names often have in the Old Testament?

3. When Moses asked God at the burning bush by what name he should be called, how did God answer?

4. What was significant about the name Joseph was told to give Mary's baby? What other prominent Israelite leader had the same name?

5. Is it correct to call the Messiah's birth a "virgin birth"?

6. When was the prophecy in Isaiah 7:14 fulfilled?

7. How does Joseph signify that Mary's child will be his "son"?

8. What legal requirement does the adoption of Jesus by Joseph satisfy?

REFERENCES

New English Bible, Oxford University Press – Cambridge University Press, 1970 (NEB)

King James Version (KJV)

The Message (MSG)

New International Version (NIV)

New American Standard Bible, The New Open Bible Study Edition, Copyright 1990 by Thomas Nelson, Inc. (NAS)

The Birth of the Messiah, Raymond E. Brown, Doubleday and Company (1977) ISBN: 0-385-05907-8 (Brown)

All Bible references are NIV unless noted otherwise.

CHAPTER 4

1. Genesis 12:3
2. John 8:53
3. Genesis 17:3-5
4. Genesis 17:17
5. Genesis 27:36
6. Genesis 32:28
7. Exodus 3:13-14
8. Hebrews 11:16 NEB
9. John 14:6 NEB
10. *Mahatma Gandi's Ideas*, C.F. Andrews, Page 93
11. Luke 19:10
12. Colossians 4:11 NEB
13. Acts 4:12 KJV
14. Matthew 5:17
15. Brown Chapter IV
16. Brown Page 97
17. Genesis 3:15 NAS
18. Matthew 28:20

CHAPTER 5

WHAT IS A MAGI?

"The Supreme Court has ruled that they cannot have a nativity scene in Washington, D.C. This wasn't for any religious reasons. They couldn't find three wise men and a virgin." Jay Leno.

Matthew 2:1-8 **¹After Jesus was born in Bethlehem in Judea, during the time of King Herod, Magi from the east came to Jerusalem ²and asked, "Where is the one who has been born king of the Jews? We saw his star in the east and have come to worship him." ³When King Herod heard this he was disturbed, and all Jerusalem with him. ⁴When he had called together all the people's chief priests and teachers of the law, he asked them where the Christ was to be born. ⁵"In Bethlehem in Judea," they replied, "for this is what the prophet has written:⁶ "'But you, Bethlehem, in the land of Judah, are by no means least among the rulers of Judah; for out of you will come a ruler who will be the shepherd of my people Israel.'" ⁷Then Herod called the Magi secretly and found out from them the exact time the star had appeared. ⁸He sent them to Bethlehem and said, "Go and make a careful search for the child. As soon as you find him, report to me, so that I too may go and worship him."**

An obscure village in Judea is about to be "put on the map". At the beginning of Chapter 2, Matthew tells his readers that Jesus was born in Bethlehem of Judea. He probably wrote "Bethlehem of Judea" or Judah to distinguish it from the town of the same name in Zebulun. (1) It was the home of David and was the place where the prophet Samuel had anointed him king over Israel. The word Bethlehem means "House of Bread." Bethlehem seems to be just the right place for the birth of the "Son of David"; the one who would be called the "Bread of Life".

The village is about 6 miles from Jerusalem and to this day continues to receive thousands of pilgrims. They come to visit the Church of the Nativity which is built over the supposed location of the actual birthplace[4]. The present church was built by the Roman emperor Justinian I over a cave area which served as the stables for what is assumed was the inn which according to Luke's Gospel had "no room" for Mary and Joseph.

At this point in Matthew's story some mysterious visitors to Jerusalem make their appearance. The Magi had apparently made a long journey from "the East". They did not realize that their "journey" had just begun! They would continue their trek through history making innumerable stops at plays and crèches the world over. After their death their bones would wander back and forth across Europe and Asia. Eventually these relics came to rest in an enameled shrine which sits today in the great cathedral in Cologne, Germany. (2) These bones are supposedly those of the "traditional" Magi. Surprisingly their names, or even how many Magi there were, are not given by Matthew so their precise identity is not known from scripture.

But who were these strangers from afar and what is their part in God's Christmas story?

Legend has embellished Matthew's account of the Magi in many ways. The most obvious being the commonly accepted notion that there were three visitors. This apparently coincides with the three gifts they subsequently present to the child. However, at various times in antiquity there have been 2, 4 and even 12 Magi. (3) Also as their history unfolded, they were elevated in stature from "Magi" to "Kings". This seems to

---

4   H. V. Morton tells how he visited the Church of the Nativity in Bethlehem. He came to a great wall, and in the wall there was a door so low that he had to stoop to enter it; and through the door, and on the other side of the wall, there was the church. Beneath the high altar of the church is the cave, and when the pilgrim descends into it he finds a little cavern about 14 yards long and 4 yards wide, lit by silver lamps. In the floor there is a star, and round it a Latin inscription: "Here Jesus Christ was born of the Virgin Mary." The Daily Study Bible Series Revised Edition, The Gospel of Matthew, Volume 1, William Barclay Page 25. Just as the visiting Magi bowed to worship the child, 2000 years later the pilgrim must bow low to enter the Savior's birthplace.

have been a gradual transformation and may in fact have originated from
Psalms 72:10-11 – "the kings of Sheba and Seba offer gifts and let all
kings bow down before him."

Brown quotes a classical description of the Magi which includes the
names by which they have become know to Western Christians:

> "The Magi were the ones who gave gifts to the Lord. The first
> is said to have been Melchoir, an old man with white hair and
> a long beard . . . who offered gold to the Lord as to a king.
> The second, Gaspar by name, young and beardless and ruddy
> complexioned . . . honored him as God by his gift of incense, an
> oblation worthy of divinity. The third, black-skinned and heavily
> bearded named Balthazar . . . by his gift of Myrrh testified to
> the Son of Man who was to die." (4)

Many of the Christmas carols we sing today (e.g. We Three Kings) reflect
the traditions which have grown up around the birth stories. The Christmas
stories and songs so widely known and loved are not always strictly faithful
to the Gospel accounts. However, they have helped to keep the birth story
of the Messiah alive for believers of every generation. But sometimes the
beautiful images recalled are like fairy tales that children learn to recite and
this was not the writer's intent. The Bible student should consider the birth
stories in the same serious light as the remaining portions of the Gospel.
Matthew's purpose is to instruct his readers about Jesus Christ.

With this in mind, it is not easy to pinpoint exactly who the Magi, the
wise men or the Three Kings actually were. "Magi" is translated "wise
men" in the KJV and Revised Standard while the NEB uses "astrologers".
In Matthew's time they were probably "a caste of wise men specializing
in astrology, medicine and natural science". (5) They have also been
described as priests indicating they had religious knowledge. However,
their connection to the star in the story points toward an interest in
astronomy and astrology.

Where did the visitors come from? "Magi" are mentioned as early as
the fifth century B.C. by the Greek historian Herodotus who describes
them as Persians. (6) Arabia and Babylon have also been proposed as
their homeland "east" of Israel. Matthew's wise men may have been
from any one of these regions, or from none of them! No one knows.
The term Magi also came to identify a profession rather than a particular
citizenship. And Magi are viewed very negatively elsewhere in the New

Testament. Simon in Samaria is mentioned in **Acts 8** as a converted magician who tried to buy the power of the Holy Spirit. Later in **Acts (Chapter 13)** Paul and Barnabas encounter Elymas, a "Jewish sorcerer and false prophet," whom Paul describes as a "child of the devil". In both of these Acts passages "sorcery" and "sorcerer" are essentially the same word translated "Magi" or "wise men".

In Matthew's birth story, however, the Magi are wise men from the east who come nobly to Bethlehem bearing gifts for the Christ child. From their homeland and because of the questions they were asking in Jerusalem, they are surely Gentiles. This seems to be their most important characteristic for Matthew.

Jesus was to say later in his ministry that "I have other sheep, which are not of this fold; I must bring them also." (7) And again, "Many, I tell you, will come from east and west to feast with Abraham, Isaac and Jacob in the Kingdom of Heaven." (8) In these passages Jesus surely refers to his calling those who are not Jews. Matthew had emphasized in Chapter 1 that the child of Bethlehem was the Son of David and the Jewish heir to David's throne. But Jesus was also the Son of Abraham, in whom "all families of the earth shall be blessed." Hence those who first sought the newly born King of the Jews were Gentiles. They had seen his sign, the star rising in the east. In sending his Son to fallen mankind, God was seeking to reconcile to himself not just his special people but all of the human race. By including Gentiles, and portraying them so favorably in a Gospel seemingly aimed at Jews, Matthew must have wanted to demonstrate this.

In Ephesians 2, Paul describes Gentiles as "uncircumcised," "strangers", "you who were formerly far off" and "aliens". All of these terms could have occurred to King Herod as he greeted the Magi in Jerusalem. And he certainly would not have guessed that the God of Abraham, Isaac and Jacob would be reaching out to people considered in those terms by Jews of his day. Whether they came from Babylon, Persia or wherever, the Magi had come from afar seeking a child they knew to be extraordinary. It is quite amazing that they would do this!

We tend to think of Matthew's Gospel as being written to Jews. But there were almost certainly Gentiles in the churches who would read his story. By the time Matthew wrote his account of Jesus, the "way" had been preached in many lands. We know Paul's missionary trips had resulted in both Jews and Gentiles accepting the Christ. (9) Matthew reaches out to those who were not Jews in his birth story to assure them they were included in God's reconciliation plan from the beginning.

Were there actually three Magi? Where exactly did they come from? Did they walk or ride camels? Were they kings or magicians? None of this really matters. If we focus on what Matthew told his readers, we know only that they were important Gentiles who traveled probably a great distance to honor (and accept) the baby Jesus. Thus was foreshadowed the plan God had from the beginning. When his Son was lifted up, he would draw *all men* to himself!

Why did the star not lead the Magi directly to Bethlehem and bypass Jerusalem? Perhaps Matthew wanted his readers to understand that nature might point seekers toward God (after all "the heavens declare the glory of God" (10)) but the details are found in the Jewish scriptures. When Herod asked the scholars who knew the Scriptures "where the Christ was to be born" they quoted **Micah 5:2** to him. (The last line reference to "shepherd of my people Israel" is apparently quoted from **II Samuel 5:2**). In John's Gospel Jesus would say "You diligently study the Scriptures because you think that by them you possess eternal life. These are the Scriptures that testify about me". (11)

The stop in Jerusalem also permitted Herod to enter the story and contribute to Matthew's message. Herod passes along the information he has been given. The Hebrew Scriptures clearly state that the Messiah was to be born in Bethlehem. But before he sends them on their way he asks the exact time the star had appeared. It is as if he is saying "you tell me what I want to know and I'll tell you what you want to know!" As Matthew's story later reveals, their answer must have been "Two years ago."

Both Matthew and Luke are very explicit about the birthplace of Jesus. Although the details in their birth stories are not precisely the same, both identify Bethlehem as the birthplace. It is important again to remember to whom Matthew is writing. Believers in his day were being confronted by Jews who objected to Jesus of *Nazareth* in *Galilee* being the Messiah. This can be seen in John's Gospel which was written after Matthew and Luke but surely reflects the common objections of the first century.

John 1:45-46 [45]Philip found Nathanael and told him, "We have found the one Moses wrote about in the Law, and about whom the prophets also wrote—Jesus of Nazareth, the son of Joseph." [46]"Nazareth! Can anything good come from there?" Nathaniel asked.

John 7:41-42 Still others asked, "How can the Christ come from Galilee? [42]Does not the Scripture say that the Christ will come from David's family and from Bethlehem, the town where David lived?"

John 7:52 [52]They replied, "Are you from Galilee, too? Look into it, and you will find that a prophet does not come out of Galilee."

In Jesus' time he was thought to have "come from" Nazareth. (In Chapter 8 we shall see how Matthew deals with Nazareth as Jesus' hometown.) Such a belief would assume he was born there. But the Gospel writers' firm testimonies that Jesus in fact "came from" Bethlehem show that he indeed met the expectations the Jews had about the Messiah.

As Brown points out Matthew seems to emphasize two different responses to the birth of the "King of the Jews". (11) On one hand the birth was readily accepted by a "righteous" Jew, Joseph, and even worshipfully by Gentiles, the Magi. Contrarily, the Messiah was greeted with alarm by other Jews ("all of Jerusalem") and the outright hostility of Herod. That *"all Jerusalem"* was disturbed at the news of the birth of a new King seems to foreshadow what Jesus would experience in his Passion when *"they all"* answered Pilate, "Crucify him!" (13) When Matthew tells the reader that Herod "called together all the people's chief priests and teachers of the law" it could be a reminder that "the chief priests and the whole Sanhedrin" would later be named by Matthew as the Jewish body who condemned Jesus to the cross. (14).

Thus as Matthew's Gospel unfolds we continue to see two responses to the proclamation of Jesus as Messiah and King: acceptance and homage by his disciples and rejection and persecution by his enemies. By the time Matthew writes his Gospel, probably 30-40 years after the events he describes, Christians were experiencing the hostility of the authorities which Jesus had predicted. (15) His audience doubtless wondered why the Jews who had the Scriptures which "testify about me" largely rejected Jesus as Messiah. They probably also questioned the hostility and outright persecution they were experiencing especially from Jewish leaders. Matthew's Gospel says "don't be surprised!" It was like that during his ministry and in fact started with his birth!

When the Magi reached Jerusalem, they asked for the whereabouts of the one "who has been born king of the Jews". It is interesting, and even ironic, to realize there is only one other time Jesus is called "King of the Jews". That was when this title was placed at the top of the cross on which he was crucified and John's Gospel tells us it was again a Gentile who gave him the title: Pontius Pilate! (16)

When Herod sends the Magi on their way to Bethlehem, he instructs them to report back to him "so that I too may go and worship him." Matthew emphasizes Herod's villainy by showing he lied about his true intentions.

QUESTIONS—CHAPTER 5

1. Why does Bethlehem seem to be the appropriate place for the birth of the Messiah?

2. How do we know there were three Magi who visited Bethlehem?

3. Why are the stories and songs associated with Christmas valuable to Christians even though they are not always in accordance with the scripture?

4. Were the Magi actually kings?

5. For Matthew's purposes, what is the most important characteristic of the Magi? How does this characteristic fit into his birth story?

6. Why did the Magi have to stop in Jerusalem?

7. Where did many in Jesus time think he came from? How does Matthew's birth story respond to this?

8. What two responses to Jesus are illustrated by the events related in Matthew's birth story?

REFERENCES

New English Bible, Oxford University Press – Cambridge University Press, 1970 (NEB)

King James Version (KJV)

The Message (MSG)

New International Version (NIV)

New American Standard Bible, The New Open Bible Study Edition, Copyright 1990 by Thomas Nelson, Inc. (NAS)

The Birth of the Messiah, Raymond E. Brown, Doubleday and Company (1977) ISBN: 0-385-05907-8 (Brown)

The Interpreter's Dictionary of the Bible in Four Volumes (1962) (Interpreter's)

All Bible references are NIV unless noted otherwise.

CHAPTER 5

1. Joshua 19:15
2. Brown Page 197
3. Brown Page 198
4. Brown page 199
5. NAS (Footnote on Matthew 2:1)
6. Interpreter's Volume 3 Page 222
7. John 10:16 NAS
8. Matthew 8:11 NEB
9. Acts 17:4 NEB
10. Psalms 19:1
11. John 5:39
12. Brown Pages 213-214
13. Matthew 27:22
14. Matthew 26:59
15. Matthew 10:17-18
16. John 19:19

CHAPTER 6

STAR STRUCK!

Had the three wise men been three wise women, they'd have asked directions, arrived on time, helped to deliver the baby, cleaned the stable, made a casserole and brought practical gifts!

Matthew 2:9-12 ⁹After they had heard the king, they went on their way, and the star they had seen in the east went ahead of them until it stopped over the place where the child was. ¹⁰When they saw the star, they were overjoyed. ¹¹On coming to the house, they saw the child with his mother Mary, and they bowed down and worshiped him. Then they opened their treasures and presented him with gifts of gold and of incense and of myrrh. ¹²And having been warned in a dream not to go back to Herod, they returned to their country by another route.

One of the most enduring symbols of Christmas is the Star of Bethlehem. The Magi reported in Jerusalem that they had seen "his star in the east". The star with "royal beauty bright" has been immortalized as the compass which guided the eastern "kings" to the stable where the child lay. The vision of a brilliant heavenly body coursing through the sky as God's own beacon is wonderful! It has inspired poets and enchanted children throughout the ages. Today it reappears in December of every year over suburban landscapes and atop evergreen trees in hundreds of shopping malls. (It might be observed that while it originally led wise men to *bring* gifts it now inspires the less wise to *buy* gifts!) But is it more than just a divine ornament decorating the greatest story ever told?

If God wanted Gentiles to have a part in the birth story of the Messiah, perhaps he needed a way to signal them. In any case, wise men, who were not Jewish, responded to what they understood to be a divine sign.

Many intense efforts have been made to identify the star. It has been variously speculated that the wise men saw a meteor, or a comet or a nova or a supernova. Various planets have been suggested. Calculations by the great physicist Kepler indicate Jupiter and Saturn were close by each other (in conjunction) two years before the birth of Christ. (1) The timing and magnificence of this display has led some to believe this pairing of planets to be "his star". For Magi in an Eastern land who took astronomy and astrology very seriously, the appearance of this conjunction could have so aroused their attention that they went off searching for its significance. Edersheim reports an "evanescent star" appears in ancient Chinese astronomical tables, which was designated by others as a comet. This comet's first appearance was "calculated" to coincide with "his star's" appearance and even its location and movement was "astronomically ascertained" to support Matthew's account. (2)

It has been noted that there were expectations at this time that a ruler would soon come out of Judea. The Roman historian Suetonius wrote, "There had spread over all the Orient an old and established belief that it was fated at the time for men coming from Judea to rule the world." (3)

It has further been noted in various places that the births of great men were heralded by extraordinary displays in the heavens. The implication is that neither Matthew's readers nor Magi who watched the skies would be surprised by a special star announcing a special event.

A careful reading of Matthew's account tells us the Magi "saw his star in the east" (or "rising" in some versions). It does not say they followed it to Jerusalem. In the time preceding Jesus' birth there were many Jewish communities in the eastern lands from which the Magi came. If an extraordinary sight in the heavens had aroused their curiosity, they could have made inquiries in these Jewish settlements. They might have learned of the Jewish expectations for a glorious King to rule the world. Jerusalem was the capital of Israel and would be the logical place to ask about "one born to be king of the Jews".

After they met with Herod, Matthew writes "the star they had seen in the east went ahead of them until it stopped over the place where the child was." Matthew does not seem perturbed by the erratic and uncharacteristic movement of "his star"! Heavenly bodies we would think of as stars do not behave as this one did. Further, its prominence and strange movements (apparently including a "ray" or "beam" which identified the precise "place where the child was") seem to have gone unnoticed by the general populace.

It is possible that what the Magi saw was not really a known star in the cosmos. They called it "his star". Perhaps its appearance was unique to his birth. In Isaiah's prophecy Israel was to be a "light for the Gentiles". (4) At the birth of Israel's Messiah, his light attracted Gentiles. This suggestion, the possibility that God crossed over from his realm into human history and announced the arrival of his Son has been linked to the **Shekinah.** (5) In the Old Testament, God signaled his presence on various occasions by special manifestations of light. When Moses guided the Israelites out of Egypt, God actually led them by a "pillar of fire". (6) This "pillar of fire" moved before them and guided them much as "his star" did for the Magi. The first time Moses was on Mt. Sinai "the glory of the LORD looked like a consuming fire on top of the mountain." (7) When the tabernacle was completed, the glory of the Lord filled it in the form of a fire "in the sight of all the house of Israel during all their travels." (8)

The prophet **Ezekiel** writes about a spectacular vision of the glory of God in the **first Chapter** of his book and concludes the section saying, "This was the appearance of the likeness of the glory of the LORD." (9) In **Chapter 10 Ezekiel** continues his description of the glory of God: "Then the Glory of God left the Temple entrance and hovered over the cherubim. I watched as the cherubim spread their wings and left the ground, the wheels right with them. They stopped at the entrance of the east gate of the Temple. The Glory of the God of Israel was above them." (10) Finally the glory of God left Jerusalem and departed toward a mountain to the east. "The glory of the LORD went up from within the city and stopped above the mountain east of it." (11)

This movement of the glory of God characterized by intense brightness sounds very similar to the star's behavior in Matthew's story. The Jews had a term for this appearance of God, this presence of God, often in the form of brilliant light. It was called the **Shekinah.** Although the term is not used in the Old Testament, the ancient Hebrews recognized the Shekinah glory of God as his dwelling with his people. When the Shekinah disappeared to the east of Jerusalem in **Ezekiel Chapter 11**, it did not appear again in Old Testament times. And then hundreds of years later in Matthew's birth narrative a "star" rose in the east.

As with the Magi, the details of "his star" are not knowable to us. Exactly what it was is impossible and unnecessary to know. God was at work identifying that his son was born and he took special measures to make sure the world knew he was inviting Gentiles to the celebration. That seems to be Matthew's point.

The Magi follow the star which leads them to "the place where the child was". The account says they were overjoyed when they saw the star rather than overjoyed when they saw the child. This indicates that the reappearance of the "star" which had started them on their search now confirms that they have found the child they had been seeking! When they see the child, they bow, worship and present their gifts. It is a startling contrast to the attitudes of the "chief priests and teachers of the law" who could have followed the path to Bethlehem. The Jewish leaders had the Scriptures and knew the Scriptures. But they still missed the arrival of the Messiah. It is also a striking contrast to Herod's murderous anger! Again, these attitudes are simply previews of what Jesus will experience during his preaching ministry.

Since there are three gifts mentioned, there must have been three Magi. Or so the argument goes! Gold is still a welcome gift at Christmas time whether it be earrings, ring or watch. But myrrh and frankincense don't exactly fly off department store shelves during the holiday shopping season. However, in New Testament times these would have been valuable gifts and the three gifts might have financed the upcoming trip to Egypt.

Gold has always been precious and considered the suitable gift for a king. The furnishing and decorations specified for the tabernacle (God's dwelling place) were to be gold and gold overlay. The term "pure gold" is used repeatedly in the building instructions for God's "house". This gift clearly signifies that the Magi are convinced they are bowing before the "King of the Jews'.

Frankincense came to Palestine from Arabia and was an appropriate gift offered by visitors from the East. It is a fragrant gum resin which is ground into powder and when burned gives off a balsam-like odor. According to the instructions given to Moses, frankincense was a main ingredient of the incense which was to be holy unto the Lord. And this incense was to have only one use: "Do not make any incense with this formula for yourselves; consider it holy to the LORD. Whoever makes any like it to enjoy its fragrance must be cut off from his people." (12) Frankincense was set before the holy of holies with the Bread of Presence.

(13) It came to symbolize the prayers of God's people ascending to heaven and to represent the office of the priesthood.

Myrrh, like frankincense, was also a fragrant resin which came from the trunk and branches of small trees growing in Arabia. It was considered an especially prized product of the region from which the Magi came and may have pointed to their homeland. It was used as perfume as in **Proverbs 7:17** and **Psalm 45:8**. Matthew's emphasis was probably elsewhere. Although he does not mention myrrh again in his Gospel, his intent was probably to anticipate the death of Jesus. It is the only one of the gifts that Jesus was known to receive again. In Mark we read that Jesus' executioners "offered him wine mixed with myrrh, but he did not take it" as he was hanging on the cross. (14) John's Gospel tells us that Nicodemus brought myrrh as an embalming material to the Lord's lifeless body. (15)

Matthew describes the gifts brought to Jesus at his birth because, like in the rest of his Gospel, he writes to inform his readers who he is. Gold identifies the child of Bethlehem as king, *the* king not a king! Jesus' earliest proclamation was that the "kingdom" had arrived. (16) It had arrived because the king had arrived.

Frankincense reminds the reader of the priesthood. When the priest entered the Holy of Holies and when he offered the sacrifices, he was connecting the people to God. When Jesus offered himself as the ultimate sacrifice, he was opening the way for man to enter God's presence. "And, once made perfect, he became the source of eternal salvation for all who obey him and was designated by God to be high priest in the order of Melchizedek." (17)

Myrrh would be associated with death. The one born to be king and high priest was also born to die. This gift reminds the reader that God's plan from the beginning was that he would "give his only begotten son" in death. Paul writes about this in Romans: "But God demonstrates his own love for us in this: While we were still sinners, Christ died for us." (18) Mankind's ultimate experience, the one which is always in the background of life's experiences, is death. Life for most is a mixture of joy and sorrow with the prospect of death always present. "Just as man is destined to die once, and after that to face judgment, so Christ was sacrificed once to take away the sins of many people; and he will appear a second time, not to bear sin, but to bring salvation to those who are waiting for him." (19) Just as our life has joy and sorrow, life and death, so did Jesus' life. At the celebration of his birth, the myrrh reminds us Jesus would be fully human and that would include sharing our ultimate experience.

When the Magi prepared to return to their own country, they were warned in a dream not to include Herod in their travel plans! Five times in his short narrative Matthew relates that the characters in his drama were contacted by God through dreams. On three of these occasions "an angel of the Lord" appeared as God's messenger to Joseph. Now in the Old Testament many men had extraordinary dreams and often these included messages from God. Abimelech, Jacob, Laban, Joseph, the Baker and Cupbearer who shared a prison cell with Joseph in Egypt, Pharaoh, Solomon, Nebuchadnezzar and Daniel were all dreamers. Consequently Matthew would not have thought it unusual for God to orchestrate the birth of his son by directing the main participants through dreams. It was just further evidence that the Father was in firm control. Dreams with divine messages do not seem to be very much a part of the modern day Christian's spiritual life. However, it is interesting to note that missionaries in the Muslim world especially are relating stories of converts encountering Christ in special dreams. In the 21st century we have many marvelous means of communicating, but maybe God prefers the "old ways"!

QUESTIONS—CHAPTER 6

1. What led the Magi to Jerusalem?

2. What possibilities have been suggested to explain the star which aroused the interest of the Magi?

3. Why was gold an appropriate gift for the baby Jesus?

4. What was the glorious presence of God in the form of brilliant light called by Jewish scholars?

5. How did God convey his messages to the characters in Matthew's narrative?

6. What role did the frankincense brought by the Magi as a gift to the child come to symbolize? Why?

7. Which gift brought by the Magi was Jesus known to have been offered late in his life?

8. What practical purpose could the gifts brought by the Magi have served?

REFERENCES

New English Bible, Oxford University Press – Cambridge University Press, 1970 (NEB)

King James Version (KJV)

The Message (MSG)

New International Version (NIV)

The Birth of the Messiah, Raymond E. Brown, Doubleday and Company (1977) ISBN: 0-385-05907-8 (Brown)

The Life and Times of Jesus the Messiah—Alfred Edersheim MacDonald Publishing Company ISBN 0-917006-12-7 (Edersheim)

All Bible references are NIV unless noted otherwise.

CHAPTER 6

1. Edersheim Vol 1 page 212
2. Edersheim Vol 1 page 213
3. Quoted by many sources; originally from "Life of Vespasian"
4. Isaiah 42:6
5. "Return of the Star of Bethlehem" (Boa and Proctor) as excerpted in the Christian Reader Nov.-Dec 1988
6. Exodus 13:21
7. Exodus 24:17
8. Exodus 40:38
9. Ezekiel 1:28
10. Ezekiel 10:18-19 MSG
11. Ezekiel 11:23 MSG
12. Exodus 30:34-37
13. Leviticus 24:7
14. Mark 15:23
15. John 19:39
16. Matthew 4:17
17. Hebrews 5:9-10
18. Romans 5:8
19. Hebrews 9:27-28

CHAPTER 7

EXODUS! AGAIN!

"When the Lord sends tribulation, He 'spects us to tribulate."
-Unnamed Southern preacher

Matthew 2:13-16 **[13]When they had gone, an angel of the Lord appeared to Joseph in a dream. "Get up," he said, "take the child and his mother and escape to Egypt. Stay there until I tell you, for Herod is going to search for the child to kill him." [14]So he got up, took the child and his mother during the night and left for Egypt, [15]where he stayed until the death of Herod. And so was fulfilled what the Lord had said through the prophet: "Out of Egypt I called my son." [16]When Herod realized that he had been outwitted by the Magi, he was furious, and he gave orders to kill all the boys in Bethlehem and its vicinity who were two years old and under, in accordance with the time he had learned from the Magi.**

In another dream sequence the angel instructs Joseph to take his family to Egypt to protect Jesus from Herod. Herod would not have power to harm the baby in Egypt. This country had been a refuge before. Jeroboam had fled to Egypt when his father, Solomon, tried to kill him. (80).

In succeeding years, several strands of Christian tradition grew up around the families' visit to Egypt. One charming story originated about 225 miles south of Cairo at the monastery Deir el-Muharraq where the family is said to have lived for six months. They were attacked while there by two robbers who tried to plunder them. However, one repented when he saw Mary's tears. These two turned out to be the two thieves who were later crucified with Jesus at Calvary and the one who repented was the Good Thief. It was here, as the story goes, that the family learned what Herod had done in Bethlehem. (1)

Matthew's purpose in reporting that the family of the Messiah had gone to Egypt seems to be to link Jesus with the prophecy from **Hosea 11:1**. In this passage, God is denouncing Israel for turning from him to serve false gods. This, in spite of his love and deliverance of them: "when Israel was a child, I loved him and out of Egypt I called my son." In referring to Israel as "my son" God is emphasizing the closeness between himself and his chosen people.

This calling of Israel out of bondage in Egypt is known as the Exodus. It includes all the mighty acts of Jehovah in delivering his people from their servitude. It began with the Passover when the angel of death killed the first born sons of Egypt but passed over and spared the Jewish households. It included him leading the people safely through the miraculously parted Red Sea and going before them in the form of a cloud by day and fire by night. When the people's faith failed, God led them through wilderness for 40 years. On Mt Sinai, their leader, Moses, received the Ten Commandments and God went before them as they crossed the Jordan River and conquered the Promised Land, the land of Canaan. Thus, the Exodus was the single most important event, or series of events, in the history of Israel. It was the Exodus experience which established the identity of the Jewish people and the foremost sacrament of the Exodus, the Passover Supper, is celebrated by Jews everywhere to this day.

When Hosea quotes God as saying "out of Egypt I called my son" figurative language is being used. God called or led his people Israel out of Egypt but he refers to them as "my son". Some would understand this statement as a prophecy of what he would do further down the stream of time for his "only begotten son" although in its Old Testament context it is a statement of what God has done for His people.

Matthew sees the family coming out of Egypt as the reenactment by the Messiah of a prophetic action of God hundreds of years earlier. The Gospel writer wants his readers to see Jesus' journey into and out of Egypt as linking the carpenter of Nazareth with the most crucial event in Israelite history. What could be more evocative of the past than for "Joseph" to go once again down into Egypt just as Jacob's son, Joseph, had done centuries earlier! And Jesus' "father" Joseph comes out of Egypt just as Joseph, the son of Jacob, came out of Egypt when Moses takes his bones with the Israelites as they journeyed to the Promised Land. (2)

Again we seek to understand what Matthew is telling us about Jesus. He seems to say, "Look, Jesus is so much the promised Messiah of Israel, so much the King of the Jews, so much God's son that he is called out of Egypt just as God called Israel out of Egypt. In his infancy he is reliving God's mightiest act on behalf of his people. How could he not be the Promised One!"

Whenever "Herod" is mentioned in the Bible confusion comes along side. This is because "Herod" appears several times as a ruler in the New Testament and many were called by the same name! History has proclaimed the Herod who was "outwitted by the Magi" as Herod the Great. His son was Antipas and succeeded "the Great" as Roman governor of Galilee. Antipas was responsible for the imprisonment and beheading of John the Baptist. He was also the Herod to whom Pilate sent Jesus during his trial preceding the crucifixion.

Still another Herod appears in **Acts Chapter 12**. This was Agrippa, Herod the Great's grandson, who was named ruler over all of Palestine by the Roman emperor Caligula. He persecuted early Christians, putting James to death and imprisoning Peter. He was struck down by an angel of the Lord, was eaten by worms and died. The apostle Paul appeared before Agrippa's son, Agrippa II, in **Acts Chapters 25 and 26**. He accused Paul of trying to make him a convert to Christianity.

Another son of Herod the Great, Herod Archelaus, was reigning in Judea when Joseph brought his family back to Israel from Egypt, so they went to Galilee. Yet another son, Herod Philip is mentioned as a tetrarch in **Luke 3:1**. These two sons were rulers over parts of the territory previously under the domain of Herod the Great.

Herod the Great was a prominent figure on the world stage of his time. He ruled from 37 BC until 4 BC. He connived with and cajoled the most powerful men (and women) in the world including Cassius, Antony, Octavius (Augustus), and Cleopatra. His relationships with Roman emperors were necessary because Palestine was a Roman province and Herod ruled at their pleasure.

Herod had ten wives and some might consider him "Great" for this reason alone! However this title flows mostly from his accomplishments as a builder. His most notable achievement was the rebuilding of the temple in Jerusalem which was begun in 20 B.C. Rabbinic literature says: "He who has not seen the Temple of Herod has never seen a beautiful building." (3) He also built himself a royal palace, fortresses, temples and the port city of Caesarea.

Herod's political career was marked by constant battles and intrigues to keep himself in power. He tried to ally himself with the 'winners' in Rome and when he didn't choose the right side, he used his army, his influence, his alliances and his powers of persuasion to stay on top. This was his mindset when the Magi inquired about "the one who has been born "king of the Jews"". It is not surprising that he had little interest in Jesus as the predicted Messiah. He would have been focused on eliminating a rival to his power.

Having ten wives in not really the path to a stable home life! Herod's domestic life was one of almost constant turmoil. His preoccupation with holding onto power caused him to be suspicious of everyone around him. He killed rivals and perceived rivals alike. This murderous vein in his character extended even to his close family. He arranged the death of his favorite wife, Mariamne, when he thought she plotted against him. Because he loved her, he never fully recovered from this episode. He killed his two sons by Mariamne. This earned him the comment by Emperor Augustus that "it was better to be Herod's pig than to be his son!" which was a play on the Greek words for pig and son. (4)

Herod's standing with the Jewish people was mixed. Since he was only half Jewish, many considered him not qualified to be a king over the Jews. When he reduced taxes, he became more acceptable. When he sponsored Greek and Roman culture, he angered the religious leaders.

As his death approached, Herod commanded the notable Jews from all over the country to assemble in Jericho. He imprisoned them there and ordered his sister to execute them all when he died so that there would be a true time of mourning when he passed! Upon his death, she released them. (See special note about Herod at the end of this chapter.)

When the Magi made their appearance in Jerusalem, Herod was near the end of his life. He was ill from a disease from which he never recovered. He was almost 70 years old but he was still animated by the same passions. When his plan to locate the new king was foiled, he ordered the killing of the male children two years and younger in Bethlehem. Many of Herod's atrocities are mentioned in the writings of his time. This one is not. However, it is quite conceivable that this was a typical Herod reaction. It has been speculated that, based on the estimated population of Bethlehem at the time of the massacre, there would have been about 20 males 2 years and younger. Perhaps the event was barely noticed in the context of Herod's other cruel acts at the close of his life. Some writers may have omitted unsavory details of his life in order to stay in the good graces of his sons who succeeded him.

Matthew includes this detail in his birth story to make another connection between the Messiah and Israel. The **first two Chapters of the book of Exodus** relate how another ruler gave an order to put Hebrew male children to death. When the Jews in Egypt became ever more numerous in spite of the hard conditions to which they were subjected, Pharaoh ordered the Jewish boy babies thrown into the Nile River. He may have considered this to be a type of sacrifice to the river to entice it to stay in its banks during flood season. But his main purpose was to reduce the threat from his country's burgeoning slave population. The purpose of the story in Exodus is to introduce Moses as one protected by God and chosen to lead Israel out of bondage.

Moses is, of course, one of the greatest figures in Israel's history. "Condensed into this one man are the figures of prophet, priest, judge (a foreshadowing of the king), lawgiver, intercessor, victor, exile, fugitive, shepherd, guide, healer, miracle-worker, man of God, and rebel. Moses does not merely assist at the birth of Israel; in him Israel is born." (5)

When he was born, his mother feared he would be found by the Egyptians and drowned in the river. So she put him in a basket, set the basket in the bulrushes along side of the Nile and had his sister watch to see what would happen. The infant was found by Pharaoh's daughter and taken into the royal court and raised as a family member. This was all part of God's preparation of Moses for the most significant event in Israel's life story—the Exodus.

When reading about Herod killing children in Bethlehem, many in Matthew's audience would have been reminded of the similar circumstances of the birth of Moses. Not only is Jesus cast in the shadow of the great lawgiver, he is experiencing in his birth story the beginning of the formative chapter of Israel's history. When Moses receives the law directly from Jehovah, he is on the mountain. When Matthew records Jesus' sermon which expands the law (**Chapters 5-7**), he has Jesus preaching from the 'mountainside". It is with great skill that Matthew weaves the birth of the Messiah into the panorama of Israel!

Special Note

Edersheim reports the last days of Herod the Great as follows: "The cup of Herod's misdeeds, but also of his misery was full. During the whole latter part of his life, the dread of a rival to the throne had haunted him, and he had sacrificed thousands, among them those nearest and dearest to him, to slay that ghost. And still the tyrant was not at rest. A more terrible scene is not presented in history than that of the closing days of Herod. Tormented by nameless fears; ever and again a prey to vain remorse, when he would frantically call for his passionately-loved, murdered wife Marianime, and her sons; even making attempts on his own life; the delirium of tyranny, the passion for blood, drove him to the verge of madness. The most loathsome disease, such as can scarcely be described, had fastened on his body, and his sufferings were at times agonizing. By the advice of his physicians, he had himself carried to the baths of Callirhoe (east of the Jordan), trying all remedies with the determination of one who will do hard battle for life. It was in vain. The namelessly horrible distemper, which had seized the old man of seventy, held him fast in its grasp, and, so to speak, played death on the living. He knew it, that his hour was come, and had himself conveyed back to his palace under the palm trees of Jericho. They had known it also in Jerusalem, and, even before the last stage of his disease, two of the most honored and loved Rabbis—Judas and Matthias—had headed the wild band, which would sweep away all traces of Herod's idolatrous rule. They began by pulling down the immense golden eagle, which hung over the great gate of the Temple. The two ringleaders, and forty of their followers, allowed themselves to be taken by Herod's guards. A mock public trial in the theatre at Jericho followed. Herod, carried out on a couch, was both accuser and judge. The zealots, who had made noble answer to the tyrant, were burnt alive; and the High-Priest, who was suspected of connivance, deposed.

After that the end came rapidly. On his return from Callirhoe, feeling his death approaching, the King had summoned the noblest of Israel throughout the land of Jericho, and shut them up in the Hippodrome, with orders to his sister to have them slain immediately upon his death, in the grim hope that the joy of the people at his decease would thus be changed into mourning. Five days before his death one ray of passing joy lighted his couch. Terrible to say, it was caused by a letter from Augustus allowing Herod to execute his son Antipater—the false accuser and real murderer of his half-brothers Alexander and Aristobulus. The death of the wretched prince was hastened by his attempt to bribe the jailer, as the noise in the palace, caused by an attempted suicide of Herod, led him to suppose his father was actually dead. And now the terrible drama was hastening to a close. The fresh access of rage shortened the life which was already running out. Five days more, and the terror of Judea lay dead. He had reigned thirty-seven years—thirty-four since his conquest of Jerusalem. Soon the rule for which he had so long plotted, striven, and stained himself with untold crimes, passed from his descendants. A century more and the whole race of Herod had been swept away." *The Life and Times of Jesus the Messiah*—Alfred Edersheim MacDonald Publishing Company Volume 1 Page 217-218

QUESTIONS—CHAPTER 7

1. What is the significance of Jesus going to Egypt?

2. What all can be included in the term "Exodus"? What did Israel experience during their Exodus?

3. Two Israelite men with the same name went down to Egypt and both "came out of Egypt". Who were they?

4. Why was "Herod the Great" considered to be "great"?

5. How many infant boys in Bethlehem are estimated to have been killed by Herod?

6. By including the story of the killing of the infant boys Matthew links Jesus with what other prominent figure in Israel's history? What is the link?

7. Matthew connects Jesus with the same prominent Israelite later in his Gospel. Where and what is the connection?

8. "When the Lord sends tribulation, He 'spects us to tribulate". What do you think the preacher means?

REFERENCES

New English Bible, Oxford University Press – Cambridge University Press, 1970 (NEB)

King James Version (KJV)

The Message (MSG)

New International Version (NIV)

The Birth of the Messiah, Raymond E. Brown, Doubleday and Company (1977) ISBN: 0-385-05907-8 (Brown)

The Life and Times of Jesus the Messiah—Alfred Edersheim MacDonald Publishing Company ISBN 0-917006-12-7 (Edersheim)

The Zondervan Pictorial Encyclopedia of the Bible in Five Volumes (1975) (Zondervan)

The Interpreter's Dictionary of the Bible in Four Volumes (1962) (Interpreter's)

All Bible references are NIV unless noted otherwise.

CHAPTER 7

1. Brown Page 204
2. Exodus 13:19
3. Zondervan Volume 3 Page 134
4. Brown Page 226
5. Interpreter's Volume 3 Page 441

CHAPTER 8

UNLIKELY HOMETOWN!

"I like to see a man proud of the place in which he lives. I like to see a man live so that his place is proud of him."—A. Lincoln

Matthew 2:17-23 **[17]Then what was said through the prophet Jeremiah was fulfilled: [18] "A voice is heard in Ramah, weeping and great mourning, Rachel weeping for her children and refusing to be comforted, because they are no more." [19]After Herod died, an angel of the Lord appeared in a dream to Joseph in Egypt [20]and said, "Get up, take the child and his mother and go to the land of Israel, for those who were trying to take the child's life are dead." [21]So he got up, took the child and his mother and went to the land of Israel. [22]But when he heard that Archelaus was reigning in Judea in place of his father Herod, he was afraid to go there. Having been warned in a dream, he withdrew to the district of Galilee, [23]and he went and lived in a town called Nazareth. So was fulfilled what was said through the prophets: "He will be called a Nazarene."**

Matthew now refers his readers to a passage from the prophet **Jeremiah (31:15).** When Jacob returned to his mother's homeland to find a bride, he met and fell in love with a beautiful shepherdess. She turned out to be Rachel, the daughter of his mother's brother Laban. He was so taken with Rachel that he agreed to work seven years for his uncle to gain her hand. At the wedding seven years later the crafty Laban substituted his older, less attractive, daughter Leah as Jacob's new bride. When the lights came on in the morning and Jacob discovered the ruse, he confronted Laban. Laban agreed to give him Rachel also but required him to work another seven years to seal the deal! As the story unfolds, Jacob loves Rachel more than Leah and she eventually gives him his two best loved sons, Joseph and Benjamin. (See **Genesis 29** for the details of this romantic tale!)

Rachel died while giving birth to Benjamin and was buried at a site traditionally thought to be near Bethlehem. (It is marked today by a shrine originally erected by the Crusaders.) Matthew thus makes a geographical connection between Rachel's lament and the "massacre of the innocents" by Herod. Jeremiah's statement has Rachel's voice being heard in "Ramah" which is a common name in Israelite geography so that its exact location is not clear. Jeremiah's intent seems to be to refer to the passing of Israelite captives through "Ramah" on their way to Babylon. He writes in **Chapter 40** of his prophecy "God's Message to Jeremiah after Nebuzaradan captain of the bodyguard set him free at Ramah. When Nebuzaradan came upon him, he was in chains, along with all the other captives from Jerusalem and Judah who were being herded off to exile in Babylon." (1)

The captives at Ramah probably included many from the tribe of Benjamin which would have been "her children". They were being carried away to a distant foreign land and hence were "no more" in their homeland. The Babylonian captivity is dated at 586-587 BC but there were several deportations under Nebuchadnezzar. The Jewish temple was destroyed in 586 BC. Hundreds of years later Matthew has Rachel weeping again for Israelite children being persecuted in Bethlehem near Ramah.

More significant for Matthew may have been the implied reference to the second of Israel's great trials. "In the theology of Israel the persecution in Egypt and the Exile (in Babylon) were the two greatest trials to which God's people had been subjected; and the Exodus and the return from Exile were the two greatest manifestations of Yahweh's protective power." (2)

Once again Matthew's Messiah, Jesus of Nazareth, is presented as linked to and experiencing in his birth another of the most significant events in Israel's history.

This passage also illustrates again Matthew's use of Old Testament passages in a way which he terms prophecy. He writes "Then what was said through the prophet Jeremiah was fulfilled." Again what Jeremiah wrote does not sound like what we tend to understand as "prophecy". It is not an explicit prediction of some future event. "A voice is heard in Ramah, weeping and great mourning, Rachel weeping for her children and refusing to be comforted, because they are no more." The context of this statement is actually one of hope. God is speaking through Jeremiah telling Israel that although he has scattered the people to distant lands, he will bring them back and restore their fortunes. Rachel, symbolizing the people, is in distress (weeping) because the captives are being led away and because she believes they (Israel) are disappearing forever. Not so, God says! And in verses **16 and 17 of Chapter 31** he tells them what is going to happen in the future. [16]This is what the LORD says: "Restrain your voice from weeping and your eyes from tears, for your work will be rewarded," declares the LORD. "They will return from the land of the enemy. [17] So there is hope for your future," declares the LORD. "Your children will return to their own land."

While **Jeremiah 31:15** is not an explicit prediction, it is used in a prophetic context of God speaking about the future. Matthew seems to believe that the sadness of Rachel (Israel) looked forward to a distant time when her children again would be persecuted. He seems to say that just as Rachel wept for her perishing children so it is in Bethlehem where mothers are crying out for their murdered children.

Did Matthew expect his readers to know and understand the hopeful context of this passage i.e. the brutal persecution of his people would not deter God from fulfilling his plan? We do not know but it certainly seems to be a possibility. Later in his Gospel story, the disciples of Jesus would be devastated at his cruel death on the cross. But three days later his tomb was empty!

In verse 19 Herod has died. Matthew relates that an angel reports to Joseph in a dream (continuing the dream motif) that "those who were trying to take the child's life are dead". "Those" may refer to Herod and his son, Antipater. Antipater seemed to be Herod's heir but Herod put him to death shortly before he himself died, and in his will he divided his dominion among three other sons. Archelaus got Judea and apparently shared the cruel nature of his father. Augustus eventually banished him to Gaul for his brutality, giving him the shortest reign of the three brothers. Conversely, Herod Antipas, who was given rule over Galilee, had a relatively tranquil reign of 43 years and is the "Herod" appearing in the Gospel stories about Jesus. Thus Joseph is led away from the territory of Archelaus to the calmer region of Galilee.

In Matthew's birth story he relates that Jesus was born in Bethlehem, which fulfilled a Messianic prophecy found in the Old Testament book of Micah. He now gives the reader a detail which explains descriptions of Jesus which will follow in his Gospel and which will also be found in the other Gospels as well as in Acts.

In the **21st Chapter of Matthew's** Gospel the crowd exclaims "This is Jesus, the prophet from Nazareth in Galilee" and in the **26th Chapter** a maid accuses Peter saying "This fellow was with Jesus of Nazareth." Throughout his ministry the hometown of Jesus is identified as Nazareth. So, although born in Bethlehem, Matthew wants his readers to understand how Nazareth was rightfully noted as the place from which Jesus launched his ministry.

In Luke's Gospel Jesus begins his ministry in a most auspicious way:

> "He went to Nazareth, where he had been brought up, and on the Sabbath day he went into the synagogue, as was his custom. And he stood up to read. The scroll of the prophet Isaiah was handed to him. Unrolling it, he found the place where it is written: "The Spirit of the Lord is on me, because he has anointed me to preach good news to the poor. He has sent me to proclaim freedom for the prisoners and recovery of sight for the blind, to release the oppressed, to proclaim the year of the Lord's favor." Then he rolled up the scroll, gave it back to the attendant and sat down. The eyes of everyone in the synagogue were fastened on him, and he began by saying to them, "Today this scripture is fulfilled in your hearing."" (3)

It is small wonder that the Messiah would be known as "Jesus of Nazareth." (His followers would subsequently be called "the Nazarene sect.") (4) However, further in his Gospel, Matthew tells us that Jesus leaves Nazareth and goes to live in Capernaum. (5) This move was to fulfill a prophecy from Isaiah (6), but probably also resulted from his rejection by his hometown.

Following his reading from Isaiah in the Nazareth synagogue (above), Jesus noted to the crowd that it would be difficult for them to accept him since "no prophet is accepted in his hometown." When he noted how the prophets Elisha and Elijah reached out to non-Israelites to work miracles, the unfavorable comparison infuriated the people in the synagogue. They took him out to a nearby cliff intending to throw him down to his death! But he simply walked away from them. (7) Matthew reports the same or a similar experience of Jesus in Nazareth and concludes by saying "he did not do many miracles there because of their lack of faith". (8)

But Matthew cites a specific reason for the original settlement in Nazareth. The "prophets" had said He would be called a **Nazarene.** We have seen how Matthew uses prophecy in ways which often confound our modern understanding but no doubt seemed quite suitable to first century readers. In this case the question is the most difficult yet: Nazareth is not mentioned in the Old Testament and no Old Testament writer refers to the Messiah as a Nazarene.

Many explanations for Matthew's citation have been proposed. Some are very complicated as they depend on various Hebrew and Greek words around the word translated in our text as "Nazarene." This word applies to Jesus because he came from Nazareth. Matthew may have seen a similarity between "Nazarene" and the Hebrew *neser* in the passage from **Isaiah 11:1** "A shoot will come up from the stump of Jesse (the father of David); from his roots a Branch *(neser)* will bear fruit." This would further highlight Jesus' descent from David.

The letters in "Nazirite" *(Nazir)* and "Nazarene" are similar and it has been suggested that Matthew may have been linking Jesus to the rite described in **Numbers 6:1-21**. (9) Jesus was dedicated to God's service from birth, like Samson, the Nazirite. One Septuagint version of **Judges 16:17** reads [17]So he (Samson) told her everything. "No razor has ever been used on my head," he said, "because I have been a **Nazirite** set apart to God since birth." The word used for Nazirite is another Greek word which is translated elsewhere as "holy one of God". The only other Biblical character given that title, "holy one of God", is Jesus and it is applied to him three times in the Gospels.

Mark 1:24 [24]"What do you want with us, Jesus of Nazareth? Have you come to destroy us? I know who you are—the Holy One"

Luke 4:33-Luke 4:34 [33]In the synagogue there was a man possessed by a demon, an evil spirit. He cried out at the top of his voice, [34]"Ha! What do you want with us, Jesus of Nazareth? Have you come to destroy us? I know who you are—the Holy One of God!"

John 6:69 [69]We believe and know that you are the Holy One of God."

However, Jesus was certainly not a Nazirite as it is described in Numbers 6. And any connection between the words "Nazirite" and "Nazarene" is unclear.

As his ministry progressed, the association with Nazareth seems to have become an unflattering one. Initially used simply as a term of identification it became one of derision. "Nazareth! Can anything good come from there?" Nathanael asked. (10) After Jesus was taken into custody as a criminal Peter came under suspicion: As he (Peter) moved over toward the gate, someone else said to the people there, "This man was with Jesus the Nazarene." (11) The criminal was "the Nazarene"! And as seen above, it was the unclean spirits who referred to "Jesus of Nazareth". As Jesus was hanging on the cross, Pilate had the sign "JESUS OF NAZARETH THE KING OF THE JEWS" fastened over his head. When Matthew writes that Jesus would be called "a Nazarene" his intention may have been to say that he would be the despised and rejected "suffering servant" described by the prophet Isaiah. (12)

What exactly inspired Matthew to write that Jesus' being taken as an infant to Nazareth was a fulfillment of prophecy cannot be known. However, he seems to understand that the collective voice of the "prophets" (not a specific prophet) point to a Messiah who would be called a "Nazarene". These voices are sufficient for Matthew to see Jesus' home in Nazareth as part of God's plan for his son.

QUESTIONS—CHAPTER 8

1. Who are the children the prophet refers to as "her children" in Jeremiah 31:15?

2. Matthew's reference to "Rachel weeping for her children" links Jesus to what great trial in Israel's history?

3. What is the prophetic context of Jeremiah 31:15?

4. Why is Joseph told to return to the land of Israel?

5. Why did Joseph go to Nazareth instead of Bethlehem?

6. What opinion did the people of New Testament times have about Nazareth?

7. Where is "Nazarene" found in the Old Testament?

8. What are the only two characters in the Bible referred to as "holy One of God"?

REFERENCES

New English Bible, Oxford University Press – Cambridge University Press, 1970 (NEB)

King James Version (KJV)

The Message (MSG)

New International Version (NIV)

The Birth of the Messiah, Raymond E. Brown, Doubleday and Company (1977) ISBN: 0-385-05907-8 (Brown)

The Life and Times of Jesus the Messiah, Alfred Edersheim MacDonald Publishing Company ISBN 0-917006-12-7 (Edersheim)

The Zondervan pictorial Encyclopedia of the Bible in five Volumes (1975) (Zondervan)

The Interpreter's Dictionary of the Bible in Four Volumes (1962) (Interpreter's)

All Bible references are NIV unless noted otherwise.

CHAPTER 8

1. Jeremiah 40:1 MSG
2. Brown Page 216
3. Luke 4:16-21
4. Acts 24:5
5. Matthew 4:13-16
6. Isaiah 9:1-2
7. Luke 4:24-30
8. Matthew 13:58
9. Interpreters Volume 4 Page 386
10. John 1:46
11. Matthew 26:71 MSG
12. Isaiah 53

APPENDIX

STUDY QUESTIONS

AND

ANSWERS

CHAPTER 1

STUDY QUESTIONS—ANSWERS

1. *In the Gospels how many "fathers" of Jesus are mentioned? Why so many?*

Jesus is spoken of as "son of" David, Abraham, Joseph and God in the Gospels. Note: He is also the son of Mary.

Why so many fathers? Matthew uses "the son of" designation as one way to explain who Jesus is. The brilliance of a diamond is displayed when it is held up to a light. Its luster and colors are different depending upon from which angle it is viewed. It has been said that it is the same with Jesus. His brilliance depends upon from which of the four Gospels he is viewed for each conveys a different aspect of his dimension and all four are needed to complete the picture. Briefly stated "son of David" confirms Jesus as the Jewish Messiah inheriting the promises given to Israel's greatest king. "Son of Abraham" links Jesus to all mankind, "both Jew and Greek," as the one through whom all nations would be blessed. The significance of Jesus as "Son of Joseph" is discussed in Chapter 4. Watch for it there! As "Son of God" Jesus is totally unique and fully qualified for his totally unique mission. A son is often seen as the embodiment or personification of his father. Jesus said in **John 14:9** "Anyone who has seen me has seen the Father."

2. *Who is probably the most prominent human "father"?*

David is probably the most prominent human father *for the Jews*. Their greatest expectation in Jesus' time seems to be for the coming of the "Son of David", the Messiah, to sit on David's throne and restore Israel to the greatness of David's reign.

3. *What does "Messiah" mean? Why is it important as a title for Jesus?*

Messiah means "anointed". It also carries the meaning of "chosen". David was chosen as king by God and this was signified when he was anointed by Samuel. Jesus, the Messiah, was chosen by God. When Andrew encountered Jesus as described in the first chapter of John's

Gospel, he immediately told his brother, Peter, "We have found the Messiah" (that is, the Christ).

Being the Messiah (Christ) identifies him as being the one who would fulfill God's long anticipated promises. God "chose" to send his only begotten son as the Christ!

4. *What great promise did God make to David? Did God keep his promise? How?*

God said to David "Your house and your kingdom will endure forever before me; your throne will be established forever." **2 Samuel 7:16:** While David was on the throne of Israel his rule was God's rule. When Israel was taken captive by Babylon, David's hereditary, earthly rule ended. God did continue to rule in the hearts of many of the captive Israelites and they eventually returned to their homeland. When Jesus was baptized, Matthew, Mark and Luke all report a voice came from heaven, identifying Jesus as God's special chosen one: "This is my beloved Son." At the transfiguration the voice from heaven adds "Listen to him". **Mark 9:7:** Thus Jesus is identified as God's anointed one in the tradition of David. When Jesus goes forward in his teaching ministry, he uses parables extensively and these are mostly about the kingdom. The kingdom is at hand because the king has arrived.

5. *Both David and Jesus were anointed as kings by God. How does Jesus' kingdom differ from David's kingdom?*

David's kingdom was established by his military power and wealth as are all earthly kingdoms. And it faded as all earthly kingdoms do. Jesus' kingdom was established by his teaching (he was the "Word') and by his death on the cross and by his resurrection. His kingdom is eternal. David ruled as Israel's earthly king in the affairs of men. Jesus rules in the hearts of men as their eternal king.

6. *Why did God choose Abram to be the ancestor of Israel? What term describes God's action?*

We do not know why God chose Abram. When God bestows his undeserved favor, it is called grace.

7. *God made a promise to Abram which had three parts. What were they? Has God kept these promises?*

God promised Abram that he would have descendants as numerous as the stars in heaven. **Genesis 15:50**. He also promised to give him and his descendants a land of their own. **Genesis 15:7, 18**
God promised in **Genesis 12:3** that "all peoples on earth will be blessed through you."
God kept his promises. When the Israelites came out of Egypt, the men over 20 years old alone numbered 603,550. **Numbers 1:46:** The Israelites crossed the Jordan River and, under the leadership of Joshua and with God's power, took possession of the land God had promised. It is through Jesus, son of Abraham, that all people find eternal blessing.

8. *Abram evidently thought God needed help in fulfilling his promise to give him descendants. How did he try to help God?*

To help God fulfill his promise of unlimited descendants Abraham first sought to adopt his servant Eliezer and thus make him his heir. God rejected this "help" and repeated his promise to Abraham that he would have a son. When more years passed and Abraham and Sarah remained childless, Abraham conceived a son with Haggar, Sarah's maid servant, again thinking Ishmael would fulfill the promise. But God said "no" and again promised a son for the couple.

9. *Why did God wait until Sarah was 90 years old and Abraham was 100 before giving them the promised son?*

The scriptures don't explicitly say why God waited until the couple was so old before Isaac was born. But it is probably correct to infer that this timing vividly demonstrated that the creation of a special people was wholly God's work—God was acting to bring about his purposes. The child could not have been born without God's direct intervention.

10. *In the Old Testament Abraham is seen as the one who received God's promises which were fulfilled in God's people, Israel. In the New Testament, what new significance does Abraham take on?*

In the New Testament Abraham is recognized as the supreme example of faith. He is the "star" of the faith Hall of Fame in **Hebrews Chapter 11**. He above all others showed what it means to fully trust God, especially when the outcome of this trust seems so devastating.

CHAPTER 2

STUDY QUESTIONS—ANSWERS

1. *What is particularly unusual about Matthew's genealogy?*

Matthew's genealogy includes women. Women are almost never mentioned in Jewish genealogies.

2. *What do the women mentioned in the genealogy share in common? What might be significant about what they have in common?*

Three of the women mentioned would have been considered to be especially sinful and Ruth was a Moabite making her questionable. Perhaps this is Matthew's way of emphasizing Jesus' mission to save sinners and would preview his later explanation of his name. However, many of the men in the list could have made the same illustration as could all of us!

Four of the women were most probably Gentiles. Matthew may have been pointing to Jesus as a blessing to all nations—"whoever believes in him shall not perish but have eternal life".

Women might have been included in the list of Jesus' ancestors to show that he was elevating women (beginning with Mary!) to a higher status than they typically enjoyed in the patriarchal Jewish community.

Paul would later write: "In Christ's family there can be no division into *Jew and non-Jew*, slave and free, *male and female*. Among us you are all equal. That is, we are all in a common relationship with Jesus Christ." **Gal 3:28 (MSG)**

Perhaps the most compelling explanation for these women's presence in the genealogical list has to do with scandal. There was scandal associated with Mary's pregnancy when her condition appeared at an inappropriate time in her relationship with Joseph. Matthew will eventually show that Jesus' conception was not tainted. But the four women mentioned by Matthew, in addition to Mary, seem to indicate that personal scandal or questionable backgrounds do not prevent God from accomplishing his will through his chosen ones. He can use the unseemly to achieve the glorious! We should all be glad!

3. *Which of Jacob's 12 sons is given special honor?*

Of the twelve sons of Jacob, it was from Judah that the Messiah was descended. This was in accordance with the Genesis passage considered to be a Messianic prophecy by the Jews: "The scepter shall not leave Judah; he'll keep a firm grip on the command staff until the ultimate ruler comes and the nations obey him." **Genesis 49:10 (MSG)** In Revelation Jesus would be described as the "Lion of the tribe of Judah". **Revelation 5:5**

4. *If Matthew had wanted to avoid reminding his readers of the most shameful episode of David's career, he would not have mentioned what character in the genealogy?*

He would not have written of "Uriah's wife". This was Bathsheba with whom David unlawfully conceived a child and arranged for the death of her husband, Uriah, so he could have her as his wife.

5. *What character in the genealogy pretended to be a prostitute and why? Was she justified in doing this?*

Tamar pretended to be a prostitute when her father-in-law, Judah, did not provide her with a husband following the death of his son and her husband, Er. Her ruse fooled Judah and he conceived twins with her. Was she justified in her actions? Let the reader decide! But when Judah did not offer another of his sons as her husband as the Jewish law required, she took matters into her own hands and trapped Judah into giving her offspring. In her time it was a scary thing for a young woman to be left with no husband and no children. How God used her action was the point, not whether she was justified in what she did.

6. *In addition to the people listed in the genealogy what event is mentioned and why?*

Matthew includes "the exile to Babylon" in his list of ancestors. The exile is one of the most significant events in the history of Israel. It changed the nation forever. Judaism, though threatened, endured captivity and emerged with new vigor. Matthew seems to be emphasizing that Israel has risen from a very low point to its highest—from Exile to the appearance of the Messiah.

7. *What use of the number 14 does Matthew make in the genealogy? What is his purpose?*

Matthew divides his genealogy into three distinct sections each with 14 generations. For Matthew this illustrates that God is accomplishing his purposes in a planned, orderly and controlled manner.

8. *Every male in the genealogy is said to be "the father of . . ." except one. Who was that and why the change in language?*

Joseph is designated as the husband of Mary. Jesus is not his son. When Luke begins his genealogy he puts it this way: "Jesus being (**as was supposed**) the son of Joseph." **Luke 3:23 (KJV).** Joseph is not the father of Jesus in the same physical sense as the other "fathers" in the list. Although the genealogy is a list of Jesus' ancestors, Matthew is careful to emphasize that Jesus does not in fact have a human father. He is different.

9. *When comparing genealogies from different sources, what particular perspective is important to remember?*

The compiler's purpose in presenting a genealogy often shapes his selection of names to be included. Genealogies therefore do not always list exact biological ancestry.

CHAPTER 3

STUDY QUESTIONS—ANSWERS

1. *Were Joseph and Mary married when Mary became pregnant? Would it have been considered a "scandal" for Mary to be pregnant at this time?*

At the time of Mary's pregnancy, the couple had not yet had a wedding and, of course, had not begun living together. However, in the culture of the first century the betrothal arrangement was considered the first step in a marriage and Mary was legally bound to Joseph. When Mary was found to be pregnant, it was obvious to Joseph that she had been unfaithful to him. It would have been a scandal.

2. *Why did Joseph believe he could not go through with his planned marriage to Mary?*

She must be an adulteress. Adultery was a serious sin. The seventh commandment was very clear. Joseph could not marry such a woman. His dilemma was that he was "a righteous man". This implies he tried to live by God's law and that law forbid the marriage and in fact called for serious consequences for Mary. On the other hand Joseph apparently loved Mary, which led him to decide how to resolve his dilemma: he would "divorce her quietly".

3. *Is the "modern" view of adultery different than Joseph's?*

Unmarried couples living together and having children without the benefit of a wedding is viewed in our American society as nothing extraordinary. There are no reasons to believe God's commands regarding marriage and marital faithfulness have changed. But contemporary views often disregard God and his commands.

4. *What "unusual" births are described in the Bible? Was the birth of Jesus "unusual"?*

Samuel, Isaac and John the Baptist were born to mothers whose barrenness seemed to preclude their ever giving birth. In the strictest sense, the birth of these baby boys was probably not "unusual". It was their *conceptions* that were unusual and unexpected. While these women seemed unlikely to ever conceive a child, when they did, Samuel, Isaac and John the Baptist all had human fathers as do all other children. The *circumstances* of Jesus birth seem unusual to us. The star, the stable, the Magi and the angels singing to shepherds are cause for wonder! But there are no indications that the *birth* of Jesus was extraordinary. It is more correct to say the conception of Jesus was more than "unusual". It was unique. Mary surely did not doubt that she would some day be a mother. But the manner in which she came to be carrying a baby must have been totally shocking and unexpected to her. Luke reports she exclaimed "How will this be?" when the angel made his announcement to her. **Luke 1:34** For the first and only time the conception was the result of the action of the Holy Spirit instead of a human father.

5.   *When Joseph is addressed by an angel in a dream, how does the angel address Joseph? Why is this important?*

The angel calls Joseph "son of David". This further emphasizes for Matthew Jesus' identity as a descendant of David, which was a common Jewish expectation for the Messiah.

6.   *Why was Joseph's conduct when he learned that Mary was going to have a child important to Matthew's overall Gospel presentation?*

During the time Matthew's Gospel would be appearing Christians probably began using a secret symbol to identify themselves to each other and avoid detection by their enemies. This symbol was the simple representation of a fish which has reappeared in our time as a bumper sticker! The first letters of the Greek words for "Jesus Christ, God's Son, Savior" form the Greek word for fish. In the century following Jesus' ministry most Jews were rejecting the "fish words". For Matthew Joseph showed that in the very beginning a pious Jew who followed God's law had in fact accepted Jesus as "God's Son". As the birth story continues it will be seen how Matthew illustrates that Jesus was also rejected by some Jews even as he entered the world.

7. *Who is God's agent for creation?*

The great creation epic of **Genesis Chapter 1** says "the Spirit of God was hovering" as God begins bringing our world into existence. **Genesis 1:2** It is not surprising that when God brings his son into our world, it is again the Holy Spirit who is acting.

8. *Some have said the virgin birth (conception) of Jesus is not a believable story and does nothing to enhance his stature. What do you think?*

The universe which God spoke into existence is so vast that it is totally incomprehensible and unimaginable to his creatures! Is it so unbelievable that when the Son of God came into this world it would be in a totally unique way which in itself was a witness to who Jesus is? After all, it is **GOD** we are talking about here!

CHAPTER 4

STUDY QUESTIONS—ANSWERS

1. *Why did God change "the first Israelite's" name?*

The "first Israelite's" original name was Abram which means "exalted father". To confirm his promise to him that he would have countless descendants God changes Abram's name to Abraham. Abraham means "father of many". Through the centuries of Israel's history this name would be a reminder of Yahweh's promise.

2. *What significance do names often have in the Old Testament?*

Many times the name of an individual conveys something of the nature or characteristics or some other important information about the named person. Esau, speaking of his twin brother, says "Not for nothing was he named Jacob, the Heel. Twice now he's tricked me: first he took my birthright and now he's taken my blessing." **Genesis 27:36 (MSG)** Jacob means he grasps the heel (figuratively, he deceives). **Genesis 27:36** Jacob's name was changed to Israel "because you (Jacob) strove with God and with men, and prevailed." (**Genesis 32:28 NEB**) Adam means "man" and his helpmate was called Eve meaning "life" or "living" "because she would become the mother of all the living. **Genesis 3:20**

3. *When Moses asked God at the burning bush by what name he should be called, how did God answer?*

God said that Moses should tell the Israelites in Egypt that "I AM WHO I AM" has sent him. God's answer has been translated "I AM", "I WILL BE WHAT I WILL BE", "I CAUSE TO BE", "I CAUSE TO BE WHAT COMES INTO EXISTENCE" and "I AM THAT I AM" as scholars have struggled to understand God's answer. The Greek gods had easier names that rolled off the tongue like Zeus and Apollo. But God's "name" was not some simple word by which He could be defined or measured or contained. The "name" as he gives it means that any discussion of it must be approached with fear and trepidation for it seems to mean he transcends, stands above, outside and beyond all else. Man has no other word or words to describe him other than "I AM"!

⁸ "For my thoughts are not your thoughts, neither are your ways my ways," declares the LORD. ⁹ "As the heavens are higher than the earth, so are my ways higher than your ways and my thoughts than your thoughts. **Isaiah 55:8-55:9**

4. *What was significant about the name Joseph was told to give Mary's baby? What other prominent Israelite leader had the same name?*

As has been seen, in Hebrew thought names were often very important in conveying information about a person. The name "Jesus" is linked with salvation because that was his main mission. Whatever else Jesus did and taught, no matter how valuable it might be for living this life, it would not have eternal significance without his death on the cross which saved us. The Hebrew Joshua and Jesus are the same name. Joshua led the Israelites to their conquest of the Promised Land. The Promised Land may have seemed like Heaven to those who crossed the Jordan River into it. But it proved in time to be another earthly home not an eternal one.

5. *Is it correct to call the Messiah's birth a "virgin birth"?*

"Virgin birth" can be a correct term when it signifies a virgin giving birth as occurred with Mary. However, the birth process of Jesus does not seem to have been unusual. What is unique is how the conception of Jesus took place. Matthew is very clear in explaining that Mary's pregnancy was not the result of a union with a human father but was the result of the action of God's creative power, the Holy Spirit.

6. *When was the prophecy in **Isaiah 7:14** fulfilled?*

The sign that a virgin would give birth to a son was given to King Ahaz by Isaiah and since the sign was given to Ahaz it was fulfilled in his time. The sign was in the timing of the birth and not a miraculous conception associated with it. Matthew seems to see the language of the passage including reference to "House of David" as God pointing to his future action in bringing his son into our world. The "prophecy" thus has a predictive aspect which goes beyond its original message and confirms that what Matthew is writing about is part of God's long standing plan.

7. *How does Joseph signify that Mary's child will be his "son"?*

Joseph signifies that Jesus is to be his son in a "legal" sense when he takes Mary home as his wife. It must have been a great relief and joy to Mary when she realized that Joseph had been convinced that she had not betrayed him and was obviously in on her "big secret"! When Joseph gives her child the name "Jesus" as he was told to do, he further shows his determination to adopt the baby as his own.

9. *What legal requirement does the adoption of Jesus by Joseph satisfy?*

Matthew's genealogy shows that to be of "the House of David", which was a must for the Messiah, a son must have a father who is a descendant of David. But Jesus did not have a human father who was anyone's descendant let alone David's! Consequently when Jesus became a member of Joseph's household by adoption, he became a legal descendant of David.

CHAPTER 5

STUDY QUESTIONS—ANSWERS

1. *Why does Bethlehem seem to be the appropriate place for the birth of the Messiah?*

Bethlehem was closely associated with King David, probably the most illustrious ancestor of Jesus and the ancestor from whom the Jews were certain the Messiah would come. It was David's home and the place where he was anointed king. The meaning of "Bethlehem" is "house of bread". "Bread" in scripture seems to represent man's great physical need—food. Jesus was called the "Bread of Life" symbolizing his fulfillment of our greatest need.

2. *How do we know there were three Magi who visited Bethlehem?*

Matthew does not tell us how many Magi came to Bethlehem. Since there were three gifts given to the infant, the tradition of three Magi has endured although different numbers have also been proposed in the past. Matthew does not tell his readers how many Magi there were, what their names were or exactly where they came from. Perhaps he does not want us to make them into "celebrities" with individual identities. (But we did anyway!) They might become the "worshiped" instead of the "worshipers"!

3. *Why are the stories and songs associated with Christmas valuable to Christians even though they are not always in accordance with the scriptures?*

"Traditions of men" are sometimes seen as bad when they are perceived as opposing the scriptures. However, the traditions which have developed around the Gospel's birth narratives are often beautiful interpretations of the scriptural accounts which expand the stories adding worship and veneration which keep Christ's nativity alive for all generations.

4. *Were the Magi actually kings?*

Since the Magi are not mentioned anywhere in the scriptures after their appearance in Matthew's Gospel, there is no Biblical evidence the Magi were kings. However, the tradition that they were kings may be based on the passage in **Psalms 72:10-11**

[10]The kings of Tarshish and of distant shores will bring tribute to him; the kings of Sheba and Seba will present him gifts. [11]All kings will bow down to him and all nations will serve him.

It is interesting to note that many traditions which do not explicitly come from scripture do have some basis on or reference from the scriptures.

5. *For Matthew's purposes, what is the most important characteristic of the Magi? How does this characteristic fit into his birth story?*

Although almost nothing is known about the Magi, from what is said about them they are most certainly Gentiles. For Matthew they seem to signify that from Jesus' first appearance in our world, non-Jews had welcomed him and even worshiped him. *All nations* were to be blessed by Abraham's son. The Gentile believers in the early churches who were reading Matthew's story would surely have been encouraged by this early appearance of non-Jewish worshipers of the Jewish Messiah. 21st century Gentiles reading the same story can also be encouraged.

6. *Why did the Magi have to stop in Jerusalem?*

The inference is that while the Magi may have been led towards the "king of the Jews" by what they observed in nature, they could not find him without consulting the Jewish scriptures. Many report feeling "close to God" when they encounter and are touched by his majestic creation. Who has not been inspired by a dazzling array of stars in a black velvet sky or a glorious snow-covered mountain which seems to soar to the heavens! These surely witness to the existence of the Creator. But God's salvation story is written on the inspired pages of his Holy Word!

The stop in Jerusalem also allows Matthew to introduce King Herod into the birth story. And Herod will definitely play a role in Matthew's plan to explain Jesus to his readers.

7. *Where did many in Jesus time think he came from? How does Matthew's birth story respond to this?*

Since Jesus spent his early childhood in Nazareth, it was widely believed that the one claiming to be the Messiah had come from this disrespected place which could never be the home of such an honored person. Matthew will explain later in his story how Jesus came to live in Nazareth. At this point he is careful to explain that the birth of Jesus occurred in Bethlehem just as foretold in the scriptures.

8. *What two responses to Jesus are illustrated by the events related in Matthew's birth story?*

Joseph, a righteous Jew, a man of principle, accepted the incredibly miraculous birth of Jesus and adopted him into his house. The Magi, Gentiles, came a far distance to give gifts to the baby and bow in worship before him. In Jerusalem, the Jewish authorities and even the whole city seem alarmed and dismayed at the prospect of the birth of the "king of the Jews". Later King Herod will show not just rejection of the Messiah, but brutal hostility. Acceptance and worship of Jesus by some is contrasted with rejection and hostility by others. These themes are previews of the reception Jesus will receive as Matthew's Gospel continues to record his ministry.

CHAPTER 6

STUDY QUESTIONS—ANSWERS

1. *What led the Magi to Jerusalem?*

Matthew's account does not say what led the Magi to Jerusalem. They say that they saw "his star" rise in the East but Matthew does not report that the star guided them to Jerusalem. However, Matthew does say that when the Magi leave Jerusalem "the star they had seen in the east went ahead of them". This may imply that the star had led them to Jerusalem but that is unclear. The expectations in the Jewish communities scattered around the "East" that a ruler would come from Israel could have sent them to Jerusalem, the center of Judaism, when they saw the remarkable heavenly body.

2. *What possibilities have been suggested to explain the star which aroused the interest of the Magi?*

Conjunctions of planets along with comets which all appeared in the general time of the Messiah's birth have been suggested as the star described by the Magi. However, these and anything commonly understood to be a star do not behave as the star which "guided" the Magi. Perhaps it was a special manifestation of God's presence more like the "glory of God" which appeared in Israel's history in the form of brilliant light or guiding fire.

3. *Why was gold an appropriate gift for the baby Jesus?*

Gold was a traditional gift for a king so it would be right for the "one who has been born king of the Jews". God seems to consider gold to be precious. His directions for the construction of the tabernacle, his dwelling place, required that gold, pure gold, be used extensively. When Matthew's story includes the mention of this gift, he is emphasizing that his birth story is about the king of the Jews.

4. *What is the glorious presence of God in the form of brilliant light called by Jewish scholars?*

It is called the Shekinah. This word is not found in the Bible but is prominent in Jewish tradition. The word means "that which dwells or dwelling" and signifies Yahweh's presence with his people. It often came to be associated with the glory of God in turn characterized by bright light.

5. *How did God convey his messages to the characters in Matthew's narrative?*

God spoke to Joseph and the Magi in dreams. There are many instances in the Old Testament where God did this. Therefore, it would not seem unusual to Matthew's Jewish readers for God to be contacting people even Gentiles (witness Nebuchadnezzar) in dreams.

6. *What role for Jesus did the frankincense brought by the Magi as a gift to the child come to symbolize? Why?*

The frankincense gifted to Mary's child pointed to Jesus role as priest. It was used in Israel's worship to God where it was set before the holy of holies. It symbolized the prayers being offered to God and represented the role of the high priest.

The importance of Jesus as our high priest is emphasized by the writer of Hebrews who says this role enables him to sympathize with us weak creatures:

[14]Therefore, since we have a great high priest who has gone through the heavens, Jesus the Son of God, let us hold firmly to the faith we profess. [15]For we do not have a high priest who is unable to sympathize with our weaknesses, but we have one who has been tempted in every way, just as we are—yet was without sin. [16]Let us then approach the throne of grace with confidence, so that we may receive mercy and find grace to help us in our time of need. **Hebrews 4:14-16**

As the one who connects us to God the father Jesus can speak to him in our behalf: "Temptations can be strong and it is easy for them to fall. I know because I went through it." To us he can exhort: "I know it can be difficult to resist the evil one but I was there and I did it. With my help you can too!"

7. *Which gift brought by the Magi was Jesus known to have been offered late in his life?*

Matthew does not mention myrrh again in his Gospel, but Mark and John refer to it in connection with the crucifixion. It was offered to Jesus as part of a drink while he was on the cross (which he refused). John lists it in a mixture with aloes as being used to anoint his body after it was removed from the cross and this could point to its identification with death in Jesus' time. If this is true, each of the three gifts become symbols of what lies ahead for the child and represent major themes Matthew will develop in his Gospel.

8. *What practical purpose could the gifts brought by the Magi have served?*

Since the gifts were all quite valuable, they could have been sold by his parents to provide for the cost of traveling to Egypt.

CHAPTER 7

STUDY QUESTIONS—ANSWERS

1. What is the significance of Jesus going to Egypt?

When Jesus, even as an infant, goes to Egypt and returns, he becomes identified with and, in a sense, reenacts the greatest event in Israel's history. Matthew establishes this link when he introduces the passage from Hosea which he quotes: "out of Egypt I called my son". **Hosea 11:1** In the passage God refers to his bringing Israel out of their slavery in Egypt and identifying the nation as "my son". The Exodus was the greatest display of God rescuing or "saving" his people and it was the Exodus experience which forged them into a nation. For Matthew God must be doing another great thing because he again is "calling my son out of Egypt" only this time it is not Israel. It is Mary's son who has been conceived by the Holy Spirit. And this baby will be identified as God's son.

2. What all can be included in the term "Exodus"? What did Israel experience during their Exodus?

God heard his people's groaning in Egyptian bondage and sent Moses to deliver them from their captivity. It began with the Passover, an event so remarkable that it is still commemorated by Jews everywhere to this day. The Exodus also included the miraculous dividing of the Red Sea saving the people from the pursuing Egyptian army. During their journey through the wilderness God provided them with water and food in miraculous ways. He went before them as a cloud and as a pillar of fire and he came to dwell in their midst in a tabernacle. Moses, their leader, was given the Ten Commandment law, written on stone tablets by the very finger of God, on Mount Sinai. This became the basis for the covenant binding the people to God. And after 40 years of wandering God led Israel across the Jordan River to the conquest of the land he had promised them. The Exodus includes all of this!

3. Two Israelite men with the same name went down to Egypt and both "came out of Egypt". Who were they?

Joseph, the son of Jacob, was sold by his brothers into slavery in Egypt. Eventually Joseph's family followed him. And over 400 years later the great multitude of Jacob's descendants who had become Egyptian slaves was led out by Moses. Joseph, the husband of Mary, who was the mother of Jesus, goes to Egypt to escape the wrath of Herod. He soon returns when Herod dies. And with him comes not a nation but the one who will draw all men to himself.

4. *Why was "Herod the Great" considered to be "great"?*

Herod the Great ruled in Palestine for over 30 years and was involved during that time with some of the great Roman rulers of the day. At times he was esteemed by his subjects but more often he was hated by them. His greatness is most notably the result of his large and numerous building projects which included the temple in Jerusalem. Any legitimate claim to greatness Herod might have is seriously diminished by his rampant ambition which led him to numerous acts of killing and savagery even against his own family.

5. *How many infant boys in Bethlehem are estimated to have been killed by Herod?*

Because Bethlehem was not a large city, scholars have estimated that there would have been about 20 boys age two and under at the time of Herod's order. Because of this relatively small number, the tragic event may not have received much notice at the time. Also, Matthew states that Herod "gave orders to kill all the boys in Bethlehem". The extent to which the orders were actually carried out is not known. However, there is no question the orders are entirely consistent with the brutal nature of Herod.

Brown reports how subsequent Christian tradition has inflated the number of "Holy Innocents". According to his writing, the Byzantine liturgy sets the number of "Holy Children" at 14,000; Syrian calendars set it at 64,000 and by accommodation with **Revelation 14:1-5** the number has reached even 144,000 (equaling the number of "those who have not defiled themselves with women"—a safely attributed virtue at the age of two.) (The Birth of the Messiah—Raymond Brown, page 205)

6. *By including the story of the killing of the infant boys Matthew links Jesus with what other prominent figure in Israel's history? What is the link?*

When Matthew's audience reads about a ruler ordering the killing of male Jewish babies, they could have been reminded of the Egyptian Pharaoh doing the same thing 1500 years earlier. And that would have reminded them of the circumstances surrounding the birth of Moses, probably Israel's greatest leader. Again Matthew is affirming Jesus as the Messiah by linking him with Israel's lawgiver in the details of his birth story.

7. *Matthew connects Jesus with the same prominent Israelite later in his Gospel. Where and what is the connection?*

"Now when he saw the crowds, he went up on a mountainside and sat down." **Matthew 5:1** This is how Matthew begins Jesus' great teaching which has become known as "the Sermon on the Mount". In this sermon, Jesus expounds on and explains the law given to Moses on Mount Sinai. By placing Jesus on a "mountainside" Matthew seems to be pointing back to Moses.

8. *"When the Lord sends tribulation, He 'spects us to tribulate." What do you think the preacher means?*

John 16:33 (KJV) [33]These things I have spoken unto you, that in me ye might have peace. In the world ye shall have tribulation: but be of good cheer; I have overcome the world.

CHAPTER 8

STUDY QUESTIONS—ANSWERS

1. *Who are the children the prophet refers to as "her children" in* ***Jeremiah 31:15?***

Jeremiah 31:15
[15]This is what the LORD says: "A voice is heard in Ramah, mourning and great weeping, Rachel weeping for her children and refusing to be comforted, because her children are no more."

"Her children" are probably the Israelites of the tribe of Benjamin who were being taken into captivity by Babylon. Rachel was Jacob's favorite wife who died giving birth to Benjamin. She is figuratively mourning because it seems as if her "children" are disappearing forever into a distant land.

2. *Matthew's reference to "Rachel weeping for her children" links Jesus to what great trial in Israel's history?*

The second great "experience" in Israel's history (after the Exodus) was the Exile to Babylon. It was understood as God's punishment for the people's unfaithfulness. Babylon has a meaning of "the gate of gods" and was also related to "Babel" which meant "confused". **Genesis 11:9** In the Old Testament, Babylon came to symbolize confusion caused by ungodliness. Revelation in the New Testament has this description: [5]This title was written on her forehead:

MYSTERY BABYLON THE GREAT
THE MOTHER OF PROSTITUTES
AND OF THE ABOMINATIONS OF THE EARTH
Revelation 17:5

The further descriptions of "Babylon" in **Revelation Chapter 17** point to the conclusion that the term was used as a code name for Rome The Exile was also seen as the second great example of God's protection and deliverance. Many Israelites kept the faith in Yahweh alive in Babylon. And when given the freedom to return, they were led by Erza and Nehemiah back to Jerusalem.

3. *What is the prophetic context of **Jeremiah 31:15**?*

The two verses in **Jeremiah 31** following verse 15 are:
> [16]This is what the LORD says: "Restrain your voice from weeping and your eyes from tears, for your work will be rewarded," declares the LORD. "They will return from the land of the enemy. [17] So there is hope for your future," declares the LORD. "Your children will return to their own land." **Jeremiah 31:16-17**

The context is a message of hope for the future in the midst of the people's sorrow.

4. *Why is Joseph told to return to the land of Israel?*

Joseph is told that he and his family can safely return to Israel because those who were seeking to kill the baby Jesus are dead. The reason he is told to return seems to be so that the "prophecy" cited above, "Out of Egypt I have called my son," might be fulfilled. Matthew's goal of closely relating the events of his birth story to significant events in Israel's history is further accomplished. Matthew is emphatically saying "Jesus is the Messiah!"

5. *Why did Joseph go to Nazareth instead of Bethlehem?*

The text says since Archelaus who was the son of the dreaded Herod was ruling in Judea, Joseph went to Galilee instead. Another of Herod's sons, Herod Antipas, was ruling there. History appears to confirm this decision as Archelaus proves to be a cruel king and Herod Antipas showed himself more benevolent during a long reign. But Matthew sees Joseph's destination as another case of prophecy being fulfilled. The family settles in Nazareth because it had been "said through the prophets" that Jesus would be called a Nazarene. Again, Matthew's message was that regardless of what appeared to be the causes of Joseph's (and Jesus') travels, these travels were actually part of God's plan for his son.

6. *What opinion did the people of New Testament times have about Nazareth?*

During New Testament times Nazareth seems to have been a small and rather insignificant town. It is not mentioned in the Old Testament or in other contemporary non-Biblical sources. However, in Luke's birth story Mary and Joseph leave Nazareth and go to Bethlehem where the baby is born. **Luke 2:4** In Matthew's Gospel when the couple and the baby go to Nazareth, they are apparently returning there. As his ministry progresses Jesus is referred to on several occasions as "Jesus of Nazareth". (e.g. **Mark 1:24; 10:47; John 18:5; Acts 2:22**) However, the town takes on a negative connotation and seems to be held in low esteem if not out right disdain by the people in Jesus' day. Those living in Judea seemed to have a low opinion of Nazareth. "Nazareth! Can any good thing come from there" Nathanael asked. **John 1:46.**

7. *Where is "Nazarene" found in the Old Testament?*

The term "Nazarene" is not found in the Old Testament. The town of Nazareth is not found there. However, Matthew is quite comfortable saying that "So was fulfilled what was said through the prophets: "He will be called a Nazarene."" He does not cite a specific prophet or passage but refers to "the prophets". As noted in Chapter 8 he may be making a connection to "Nazirite" and/or "neser". The great prophet Isaiah wrote in his passage understood by Christians to be describing the Messiah "he was despised, and we esteemed him not." **Isaiah 53:3 (KJV).** These words sound as if they could have been used to describe someone living in the Nazareth of Jesus' time! Perhaps that is the identification Matthew is thinking of when he says the prophets have said that Jesus would be called a Nazarene.

8. *What are the only two characters in the Bible referred to as "Holy One of God"?*

Jesus is referred to as the "Holy one of God" three times in the Gospels. The great strong man, Samson, is also given this designation.

CPSIA information can be obtained at www.ICGtesting.com
Printed in the USA
BVOW05s1821190514

353962BV00001B/7/P